WEST'S LAW SCHOOL
ADVISORY BOARD

ESTATES
AND
FUTURE INTERESTS

IN A NUTSHELL

Third Edition

By

LAWRENCE W. WAGGONER
Lewis M. Simes Professor of Law
University of Michigan

THOMAS P. GALLANIS
Professor of Law and Professor of History
Director, Center for Law and History
Washington and Lee University

THOMSON
™
WEST

Mat #40410112

Thomson/West have created this publication to provide you with accurate and authoritative information concerning the subject matter covered. However, this publication was not necessarily prepared by persons licensed to practice law in a particular jurisdiction. Thomson/West are not engaged in rendering legal or other professional advice, and this publication is not a substitute for the advice of an attorney. If you require legal or other expert advice, you should seek the services of a competent attorney or other professional.

Nutshell Series, In a Nutshell, the Nutshell Logo and West Group are trademarks registered in the U.S. Patent and Trademark Office.

COPYRIGHT © 1981, 1993 By LAWRENCE W. WAGGONER
© 2005 Thomson/West
      610 Opperman Drive
      P.O. Box 64526
      St. Paul, MN 55164–0526
      1–800–328–9352
Printed in the United States of America

ISBN 0–314–16333–6

ESTATES
AND
FUTURE INTERESTS

IN A NUTSHELL

PREFACE

The objective of this book is to help law students understand the law of estates and future interests. First-year students in Property and upper-year students in Wills and Trusts are the intended audience.

It is fitting that the Nutshell Series includes *Estates and Future Interests* in its inventory of titles. It was in the future interests area that putting a body of law into a nutshell appears to have emerged. The case was *Van Grutten v. Foxwell*, [1897] App. Cas. 658 (H.L.). In the course of his opinion, Lord Macnaghten referred to Lord Thurlow's statement about the rule in Shelley's

PREFACE

Case as one that put "the case in a nutshell."[*] Lord Macnaghten added, however, that it is "one thing to put a case like *Shelley's* into a nutshell and another thing to keep it there." The warning is apt. Oversimplifying the law can be as unwise as discussing every mind-numbing nuance.

Our aim is to navigate between the two extremes. This book puts the law of estates and future interests into a nutshell, clarifying and explaining the law without oversimplification.

We wish to thank Foundation Press for granting us permission to adapt portions of Lawrence W. Waggoner, Gregory S. Alexander, Mary Louise Fellows, and Thomas P. Gallanis, *Family Property Law: Cases and Materials on Wills, Trusts, and Future Interests* (3d ed. 2002, 4th ed. forthcoming 2006), for use in the material herein, and to thank the Washington and Lee Law Review for permission to do the same with T.P. Gallanis, The

---

[*]Lord Thurlow, it should be noted for the sake of accuracy, never himself undertook to put the rule in Shelley's Case into a nutshell. His statement about the rule was contained in a letter he wrote to Francis Hargrave. The letter is published in 3 Francis Hargrave, Jurisconsult Exercitations 360 (1813).

PREFACE

Future of Future Interests, 60 Wash. & Lee L. Rev. 513 (2003).

For the production of this Third Edition, research support from the Frances Lewis Law Center of Washington and Lee University is gratefully acknowledged.

LAWRENCE W. WAGGONER
THOMAS P. GALLANIS

Ann Arbor, Michigan
Lexington, Virginia

September 2005

OUTLINE

———

OUTLINE

OUTLINE

OUTLINE

PART II. MARITAL ESTATES

OUTLINE

PART IV. POWERS OF APPOINTMENT

OUTLINE

TABLE OF ABBREVIATIONS

ALI	American Law Institute
Am. L. Prop.	American Law of Property (A. James Casner ed. 1952)
Bl. Com.	William Blackstone, Commentaries on the Law of England (1st ed. 1765-1769)
Gray on Perpetuities	John Chipman Gray, The Rule Against Perpetuities (4th ed. 1942)
IRC	Internal Revenue Code (1986 and subsequent amendments)
MMPA	Model Marital Property Act (1983 and subsequent amendments)

TABLE OF ABBREVIATIONS

NCCUSL — National Conference of Commissioners on Uniform State Laws

Restatement of Property — Restatement of Property (1936, 1940, 1944)

Restatement 2d of Property — Restatement (Second) of Property (Donative Transfers) (1983, 1986, 1988, 1992)

Restatement 3d of Property — Restatement (Third) of Property (Wills and Other Donative Transfers) (1999, 2003, 2004, and in progress)

Restatement 2d of Trusts — Restatement (Second) of Trusts (1959)

TABLE OF ABBREVIATIONS

TABLE OF CASES

References are to Pages

TABLE OF CASES

TABLE OF CASES

ESTATES
AND
FUTURE INTERESTS

IN A NUTSHELL

Third Edition

CHAPTER 1

INTRODUCTION TO ESTATES AND FUTURE INTERESTS

§ 1.1 Fragmentation of Ownership

Our legal system, like many others in the world, permits outright ownership of property. When speaking of personal property, we refer to *outright ownership* or *absolute ownership*. When speaking of land, we use the phrase ownership in *fee simple absolute*. Whatever the type of property, outright ownership carries with it several rights, known as incidents of ownership. Two important incidents of ownership are the right to possess the property (meaning the right to use it and exclude others from using it) and to transfer ownership to another

1

(inter vivos or at death).

Our legal system also permits ownership to be divided or fragmented. Derived from the English common law, fragmentation of ownership is an ingenious concept. To understand what the concept means, it is important to understand what it does *not* mean: the concept does not mean dividing property into tangible segments, each owned by a different person. (That type of division is readily possible under our legal system, but it is hardly an ingenious concept.) The ingenuity of fragmentation is that it allows two or more persons to have simultaneous interests in the property as a whole. Fragmentation of ownership involves an allocation of the incidents of ownership among the owners.

For an easy example of fragmentation, think of an apartment rented by a landlord to a tenant. The tenant has some rights to the apartment; the landlord has other rights. Who owns the apartment? The answer is that the incidents of ownership have been divided or fragmented between the tenant and the landlord. A metaphor often used to capture this idea of fragmentation is the metaphor of property rights as a *bundle of sticks*. In our example, some sticks are held by the tenant, others by the landlord.

A second example will drive home the point. Many first-year Property casebooks contain the case of *Gruen v. Gruen*, 68 N.Y.2d 48, 496 N.E.2d 869 (1986). That case concerned a father's gift of a painting to his son. The father did not give the painting outright. Instead, the father gave the son the right to possess the painting after the father's death; until then, the father retained the right of possession. The question facing the court was whether the father had made a gift during his lifetime or whether the gift occurred only at the father's death. The court held that the father had validly fragmented ownership of the painting during his lifetime. Some sticks in the bundle had been retained by the father while others had been transferred to the son.

Gruen illustrates the important distinction between *present interests* (also known as *possessory* or *present estates*) and *future interests*. It is crucial to understand these terms. A common misunderstanding is to think that the words "present" and "future" distinguish between interests that are currently created and interests that are created in the future. This is not the distinction. *Both present and future interests are already created.* That is why the court in *Gruen* correctly held that the father had made a current gift to the son: he had made a current gift of a future interest while retaining for himself a present interest.

A present interest is a right to current possession; a future interest is an interest in which possession is postponed (and depending on the terms of the future interest, possession might or might not occur eventually).

In *Gruen*, both the father and the son held interests in property. The interests were transferable and could be attached by creditors. The only distinction is that the father's interest was currently possessory, while the son's was currently nonpossessory. Put differently: the use of the word "future" in the term "future interest" refers not to when the interest is created but when (if ever) the right to possession arises. The son did not receive his interest in the future but rather at the very moment when the father fragmented the ownership of the painting.

§ 1.2　A Limit on Fragmentation: The *Numerus Clausus* Principle

The ability of property owners to fragment their interests raises an obvious question: can the fragmentation take only previously-defined forms or can owners subdivide the interests in any form they wish? The answer is that the fragmentation can occur only in a fixed number of defined forms. This is known as the principle of the *numerus clausus* (Latin for "closed number").

The principle is well illustrated by a case included in some first-year Property books, *Johnson v. Whiton*, 309 Mass. 571, 34 N.E. 542 (1893). That case concerned the interpretation of a will. The will devised property to the testator's granddaughter Sarah "and her heirs on her father's side." As we shall see in Chapter 2, this language does not correspond to any of the recognized estates. One possibility for the court would have been to say that the testator fragmented the property in a new way. But instead, the court emphasized that "a man cannot create a new kind of inheritance." Put differently: the categories of estates and future interests are fixed; the law does not recognize new forms of fragmentation.

The *numerus clausus* principle is well established in precedent, but what is its rationale? The scholarly literature on this point is not abundant.[1] We may give two answers, however. One answer is that the *numerus clausus* principle enhances economic efficiency and promotes the transfer of property. A fixed menu of options makes it easier to determine precisely which interests in property are being transferred. This in turn reduces search and transaction costs. A second answer is that the principle limits dead-hand control of property. A fixed menu prevents transferors from creating idiosyncratic burdens on property that would last long into the future.

The effect of the *numerus clausus* principle is to limit the forms of fragmentation. This has a beneficial by-product in the classroom: students need only learn a fixed number of estates and future interests, and how to recognize them.

§ 1.3 Coverage of This Book

The fragmentation of property in American law takes three main forms, corresponding to the first three parts of this book. Part I examines the

---

[1]For a recent analysis, see Thomas W. Merrill & Henry E. Smith, Optimal Standardization in the Law of Property: The *Numerus Clausus* Principle, 110 Yale L.J. 1 (2000).

temporal division of property into present and future interests. Part II examines the rights given by law to one spouse in the other spouse's property (known traditionally as the "marital estates"). Part III examines the concurrent division of property among multiple present owners ("concurrent estates").

In addition to covering these three topics, the book examines in Part IV an important device for delegating control over interests in property: the power of appointment.

Of the four topics, the most complex is the first: the law of present estates and future interests. It is appropriate to say a word about why this topic is so important.

§ 1.4   The Importance of Future Interests

The law of future interests developed in the context of interests created directly in land, known as *legal* interests because they were enforceable in the English courts of common law. Such interests are not commonly created today. Instead, future interests appear mainly in trusts.

Trusts, which often hold securities (a form of personal property) and may or may not hold land, combine two types of fragmentation of ownership. First, "legal" title to the trust property is held by the trustee and "equitable" title is held by the trust beneficiaries. These labels in quotation marks derive from England, where for many centuries the courts of law recognized the ownership of the trustee, while the Court of Chancery, administering equity, enforced the rights of the beneficiaries. The fusion of law and equity occurred in England in the nineteenth century, yet it is still conceptually accurate and helpful to think of a fragmentation of title between the trustee and the beneficiaries. Second, most trusts have multiple beneficiaries, with the equitable title divided among them in terms of time, i.e., between income beneficiaries and corpus beneficiaries. Think, for example, of a family with husband, wife, and two children. Who knows which spouse will die first? The husband and wife might each provide by will that a trust should be established for the lifetime of the surviving spouse, with the balance of the property to go at the surviving spouse's death to the then-living children. In this example, the equitable or beneficial interest in the trust is divided temporally between the surviving spouse and children.

Trusts are mainstays of modern law practice.

There are no reliable statistics about the total number of trusts in existence or about their aggregate value, because many trusts are privately created and managed. However, the federal government compiles statistics about trusts in which the trustee is a federally insured commercial or savings bank. In 2000, the most recent year for which data are available, there were 890,709 such trusts having an aggregate market value nearly $1.1 trillion.

With such wealth held in trust, most lawyers and law students should know something about future interests. Hence Part I of this book.

§ 1.5 A Word About the Hypothetical Examples Used in This Book

Hypothetical examples are used throughout this book to supplement and illustrate the text.

The hypothetical examples usually involve legal interests directly in land. This has been done to simplify the wording. As pointed out earlier (recall § 1.4), such interests are not commonly created today. Present and future interests are more commonly created in trusts of securities. Nevertheless, the process of classification is easier to understand if illustrated by examples that say "*G* transferred land to *A* for life, remainder to *B*," rather than the wordier "*G* transferred securities to the Faithful Bank, in trust, to pay the income to *A* for life, and at *A*'s death to deliver the trust assets to *B*."

Whether the transfer was a conveyance (inter-vivos transfer) or a devise (testamentary transfer) makes no difference in most of the examples. The generic word "transfer" is used in those cases. If the type of transfer makes a difference, the term "conveyance" or "devise" is used, as appropriate.

Unless otherwise stated, you should assume that the grantor, *G*, owned the property outright (i.e., in fee simple absolute) when *G* made the transfer.

The examples serve two functions. They aid initial understanding by illustrating the principles stated abstractly in the text. They also aid exam preparation by serving as review questions. Each example is arranged so that the facts and solution are given in separate paragraphs. This allows you to test your ability to answer each problem by covering up the solution, and then to check your answer.

It may help you to understand the examples if you make a linear chart of the facts as they develop over time. Starting with horizontal lines depicting the lifetimes of the transferor and transferees, insert in the horizontal lines the following symbols: ⊗ to indicate a person's death; ↓ to indicate the time and direction of a transfer; and + to indicate the time when an interest or estate of a living person changes into another interest or estate. To illustrate this technique, take a devise of land by *G* "to *A* for life, remainder to *B*." If *B* survived *A*, the case can be charted as follows:

$G{\rightarrow}\otimes$

$A{\rightarrow}\downarrow{\leftarrow}\text{(life estate)}{\longrightarrow}\otimes$

$B{\rightarrow}\downarrow{\leftarrow}\text{(remainder)}{\rightarrow}{+}{\leftarrow}\text{(fsa)}{\rightarrow}$

Your chart shows that when the life tenant, *A*, died, *B*'s remainder became a fee simple absolute.

§ 1.6 Additional Exercises (and Answers)

In addition to the examples in text, the *Nutshell* contains practice questions. The questions cover Part I; Parts II and III together; and Part IV. They are found at pages 183, 237, and 309, respectively. The answers appear in the back of the book, starting at page 311.

PART I

POSSESSORY ESTATES
AND
FUTURE INTERESTS

CHAPTER 2

CLASSIFYING POSSESSORY ESTATES (A.K.A. PRESENT INTERESTS)

§ 2.1 A Word About Classification

Classification means fixing the proper label or labels to a possessory estate or future interest. The hierarchy of estates is a refined, artificial structure that took centuries to develop fully. If it had been designed in one fell swoop, the flexibility it provides estate planners and clients of today could readily be achieved with a system of much greater simplicity.

15

The complexity and artificiality in the current system evolved, step by step over a fairly long period of time, from the struggles of competing interest groups. The owners of the great landed estates, assisted by ingenious lawyers, sought to avoid the death taxes of the day and to safeguard their estates through the generations. As one loophole was plugged in favor of enforcing the tax or promoting freer alienability and control for the recipients of the property, the ingenious lawyers found another. The result was that great distinctions were drawn on the basis of the words used in creating the dispositions. Through classification, different ways of saying the same thing were accorded different legal consequences. Form controlled over substance. In classification, form still controls over substance. Form controls legal consequences less than before, however, because the legal consequences flowing from classification gradually have been reduced.

As we study the current system, bear in mind that the system of classification, which was originally developed in feudal times mainly for legal interests in land, has been transposed today to the classification of the equitable interests in the modern trust. (See the discussions in §§ 1.4, 3.5).

§ 2.2   Three Terms of Art: Quantum, Freehold, and Particular Estate

The possessory estates are traditionally ordered in a hierarchy by *quantum*. In descending order of quantum, the groupings are: (1) fee simple estate (all fee simple estates are of the same quantum); (2) fee tail; (3) life estate; (4) term of years; (5) estate from period to period; (6) estate at will; and (7) estate at sufferance.

Feudal law in England also distinguished between *freehold* and *nonfreehold* estates. Only the former signified a lifelong bond between a free man and his feudal lord. J.H. Baker, An Introduction to English Legal History 259 (4th ed. 2002). The freehold estates are (1)-(3) above: the fee simple estates; the fee tail; and the life estate. The nonfreehold estates are (4)-(7) above: the term of years; the estate from period to period; the estate at will; and the estate at sufferance.

The term *particular estate* is a term of art denoting any estate that is less than a fee simple—a fee tail, a life estate, a term of years, and so on.

§ 2.3 The Fee Simple Absolute

The estate in *fee simple absolute* is a present interest that is not subject to termination. It is unlimited in duration. As noted earlier in § 1.1, the personal-property counterpart of the fee simple absolute is called absolute ownership or outright ownership.

At common law, a conveyance simply "to *A*" gave *A* only an interest for life. To convey a fee simple absolute, the transferor was required to include the additional words "and his heirs," as in the following example.

> *Example 2.1: G* conveyed land "to *A* and his heirs."
>
> *A* has a fee simple absolute.

The words "and his heirs" are known as *words of limitation, not words of purchase.* Words of limitation are words that act to define the estate being transferred. Words of purchase are words that transfer an interest. In Example 2.1, the words "and his heirs" do not transfer an interest to *A*'s heirs; the only person receiving an interest is *A*. The words do describe the type of interest *A* is receiving: a fee simple absolute.[1] Hence, the words "and his heirs" are words of limitation.

The words "and his heirs" were never required in wills and today are not typically required in inter vivos conveyances. A transfer "to *A*" suffices in most states to give *A* a fee simple absolute.

This *Nutshell* follows modern practice in not using the words "and his heirs" in future interests. The hypotheticals read "to *A* for life, remainder to *B*" rather than "to *A* for life, remainder to *B* and her heirs." The words do appear in hypotheticals creating present interests in fee simple—"to *A* and

---

[1]Occasionally the language of a disposition might say "*A* or his heirs." While not recommended, the substitution of the "or" for the orthodox "and" will probably not make any difference. The Restatement of Property § 27 cmts. d & e state that "or his heirs" will generally be treated as words of limitation, not words of purchase, especially when they appear in the transfer of a present interest.

A transfer to "*A* and his children" is ambiguous. *Wild's Case*, 6 Coke Rep. 16b, 77 Eng. Rep. 279 (K.B. 1599), held that if *A* has children at the time of the transfer, *A* and his children take as joint tenants (on which, see § 9.2). The rule in Wild's Case, which applied in England only to devises of land, has been repudiated by the Restatement 3d of Property § 14.2 cmt. f, which construes the transfer as creating a life estate in *A* and a remainder in *A*'s children. For an analogous result in a transfer to "*A* and his issue," see *id.*, § 14.4 cmt. f.

her heirs so long as..."—even though they are not strictly required.

§ 2.4   Defeasible Fees Before the Statute of Uses

The *defeasible fee simple* estates are subject to termination upon the happening of an event specified in the grant. Before the Statute of Uses, which we shall discuss in § 3.5, there were two defeasible fee simple estates: the fee simple determinable and the fee simple subject to a condition subsequent. Distinguishing one from another requires an understanding of defeasance.

Defeasance means loss of ownership—in other words, that the holder of the possessory interest will lose that interest upon the happening of an event that is stipulated in the grant. With respect to defeasible fees, the event stipulated in the grant is either a *limitation* or a *condition subsequent.*

The distinction between limitations and conditions subsequent is important to learn, but it is difficult for modern students because the distinction is based on the elusive contrast between grants that terminate naturally versus grants that terminate by being cut short.

Possessory interests subject to a *limitation* are understood as terminating naturally. The language in the grant signifying a limitation are words such as "during," "until," "while," "as long as," "for as long as," "so long as," "for so long as," or simply "for [a designated period]," followed by words such as "at," "upon," or "then." The limitation is called a *special limitation* if it describes an event that is not certain to happen (unlike death, which will happen eventually).

In contrast, possessory interests subject to a *condition subsequent* (also called interests subject to divestment) are understood as terminating by being cut short. The language in the grant signifying a condition subsequent are words such as "on condition that" or "provided that," followed by words such as "but if" or "and if." In some grants, only the "but if" or "and if" language will appear.

With this contrast in mind, we can return to the two types of defeasible fees mentioned in the opening paragraph of this section: the fee simple determinable and the fee simple subject to a condition subsequent. What differentiates them? The answer is that each is subject to a different kind of defeasance. The fee simple determinable terminates naturally; the fee simple subject to a condition subsequent terminates by being cut short. In formal terms, the fee simple determinable is subject to a special limitation, while the fee simple subject to a condition subsequent (as its name indicates) is subject to a condition subsequent. Consider the following examples.

Example 2.2: G conveyed land "to A and his heirs so long as A does not allow liquor to be sold on the premises; upon A's allowing liquor to be sold on the premises, the property is to revert to me."

A has a fee simple determinable. (The future interest retained by G is called a possibility of reverter. See § 3.2.)

Example 2.3: G conveyed land "to A and his heirs on condition that A not allow liquor to be sold on the premises, and if A allows liquor to be sold on the premises, then the grantor is to have the right to re-enter and take possession of the premises."

A has a fee simple subject to a condition subsequent. (The future interest retained by G is called a right of entry, sometimes called a power of termination. See § 3.2.)

To the modern lawyer, the distinction between terminating naturally and terminating by being cut short is elusive. We see nothing substantive, only minor differences in wording separating the two examples: "so long as" in Example 2.2, "on condition that" in Example 2.3. Yet the small variation in form has an important result: the present and future interests in Example 2.2 are classified differently from those in Example 2.3, and this difference in classification does trigger substantive consequences as we shall see in §§ 3.2 and 3.10. For modern students, the best advice we can give is to memorize the distinction and the sample language, above, that triggers classification in one direction or the other.

(This section has described the two defeasible fees existing prior to the Statute of Uses. For the third, see § 3.5.)

§ 2.5   The Fee Tail

The *fee tail estate* is subject to termination upon the death of the tenant in tail's last living descendant.

The fee tail estate has an interesting history, designed to preserve wealth within the great

English landed families, but its present is no longer very important and its future even less so. In almost all American jurisdictions, the fee tail estate has been abolished. Language purporting to create it—"to *A* and the heirs of his body"—has different consequences in different states. The most predominant results are that it creates a fee simple absolute in *A*, or that it creates a life estate in *A* with a remainder in *A*'s lineal descendants.

§ 2.6   Life Estates

Life estates are estates that expire naturally (by their own terms) on the death of the measuring life.

In most cases, the measuring life is the life tenant.

Example 2.4: G conveyed land "to *A* for life."

A has a life estate. The same would be true if the grant had been "to *A* so long as *A* lives," "to *A* until *A*'s death," or "to *A* during *A*'s lifetime." (The future interest retained by *G* is called a reversion. We shall study this future interest in § 3.2.)

The phrase "equitable life estate" is sometimes

used to describe the interest of a trust beneficiary who has the right to the income from a trust for his or her lifetime.

By adding a special limitation or a condition subsequent to the grant, life estates can be made prematurely defeasible, so that they might end before the life tenant's death.

Example 2.5: G conveyed land "to A for life or until A remarries."

A's estate is called a "life estate subject to a special limitation." Another name for it is a "determinable life estate." (The future interest retained by G is a reversion, which takes effect on the earlier of A's death or remarriage. Some scholars have said that G's interest that may take effect on A's remarriage is a possibility of reverter, but such scholars disagree about whether the possibility of reverter merges into the reversion. The better view is that G retained only a reversion. The reason is that G transferred out an estate of lesser quantum than G originally possessed. See the definition of a reversion in § 3.2.)

Example 2.6: G conveyed land "to *A* for life on condition that *A* not remarry, but if *A* remarries, the grantor has the right to re-enter and take possession."

A's estate is called a "life estate subject to a condition subsequent." (*G* has both a reversion and a right of entry. See the definitions in § 3.2. The reversion takes effect in possession on *A*'s death if *A* never remarries. If *A* remarries, *G*'s right of entry permits *G* to divest *A* of the remaining portion of the life estate.)

A life estate customarily arises from the inclusion of words expressly limiting the duration of the estate to a lifetime ("to *A for life*"). But a life estate can also be indicated implicitly. Consider the following example.

Example 2.7: G conveyed land "to *A* so long as he occupies the land."

Most decisions hold that *A* has a life estate subject to a special limitation, not a fee simple determinable, because *A*'s ability to occupy the land ends at *A*'s death. See Restatement of Property § 112 illus. 2.

A life estate need not be measured by the life of

the one in possession, but can be measured by the life of another. This type of estate is called a *life estate pur autre vie.*

Example 2.8: G conveyed land "to A for the life of B." A predeceases B. A's will devises her entire estate to X.

A has a life estate pur autre vie. Unlike a life estate that terminates on the life tenant's death, A can devise the remaining portion of her life estate to X. After A's death, X has a life estate pur autre vie—for the life of B.

§ 2.7   Terms of Years

Terms of years are estates that expire naturally (by their own terms) on the expiration of the term. Terms of years are defeasible estates because they are subject to a limitation ("to A for 10 years" or "to A for 30 days").

By adding a special limitation or a condition subsequent to the grant, terms of years can be made prematurely defeasible, so that they might end before the expiration of the term.

Example 2.9: G conveyed land "to A for 10 years or until A remarries."

A's estate is called a "term of years subject to a special limitation." Another name for it is a "determinable term of years."

Because a term of years is a nonfreehold estate (see § 2.2), a grant "to *A* for 10 years, then to *B*" was not characterized at common law as a term of years in *A* followed by a remainder in *B*. Rather, *B* was characterized as owning the land in fee simple absolute subject to *A*'s term of years. Today, the distinction between freehold and nonfreehold estates has little continuing importance. Characterizing *B* as owning the land subject to a term of years in *A* may still be appropriate in a commercial transaction, such as where *B*, as landlord, leases the land to *A*, as tenant. In the setting of noncommercial transactions, however, the ancient characterization was abolished in the Restatement of Property § 156 cmt. e, which states in pertinent part: "The creation of a remainder in land does not require ... that the estates preceding the future interest be freehold estates." This *Nutshell* follows the modern usage as described in the Restatement.

§ 2.8   Estates from Period to Period, at Will, or at Sufferance

These estates have little importance outside the context of landlord and tenant, and can be briefly summarized. An *estate from period to period* is "an estate which will continue for successive periods of a year, or successive periods of a fraction of a year, unless it is terminated." Restatement of Property § 20. An *estate at will* is "an estate which is terminable at the will of the transferor and also at the will of the transferee and which has no other designated period of duration." Id. at § 21.   An *estate at sufferance* is "an interest in land which exists when a person who had a possessory interest in land by virtue of an effective conveyance, wrongfully continues in the possession of the land after the termination of such interest, but without asserting a claim to a superior title." Id. at § 22.

CHAPTER 3

CLASSIFYING FUTURE INTERESTS

§ 3.1   The Distinction Between Reversionary and Nonreversionary Future Interests

The first step in the process of classification of future interests is to decide whether the future interest is a reversionary interest or a nonreversionary interest. Reversionary interests are interests retained by or created in the transferor *when the interest was created*. Nonreversionary interests are interests *created in* a transferee (someone other than the transferor).

Once made, a classification based on the reversionary/nonreversionary distinction is not altered by subsequent transfers of the interest from one person to another. So, a reversionary interest does not become nonreversionary by virtue of a subsequent transfer of that interest from the transferor to a transferee. And, conversely, a nonreversionary interest does not become reversionary if it subsequently comes into the hands of the transferor. It makes no difference whether the subsequent transfer is inter vivos, testamentary, or the result of intestate succession.

Example 3.1: G conveyed land "to A for life." Later, but while A was alive, G conveyed all his remaining interest in the land to B.

B's interest is reversionary. When G made the second conveyance, he no longer owned the life estate he had previously conveyed to A; G owned only a reversionary interest. The second conveyance constitutes a conveyance of this reversionary interest to *B*.

Example 3.2: *G* conveyed land "to *A* for life." *G* later died leaving a will that did not mention the land but contained a residuary clause devising all property not otherwise disposed of to *B*. *G* was survived by *A* and *B*.

Same result as in Example 3.1. The fact that the second conveyance occurred at *G*'s death rather than during *G*'s lifetime makes no difference.

Example 3.3: *G* conveyed land "to *A* for life." *G* later died intestate, i.e., without a valid will. *G* was survived by *A* and by his sole heir, *B*.

Same result. The fact that the conveyance to *B* occurred by operation of law (the intestacy statute) rather than by inter vivos conveyance or by will makes no difference.

Distinguishing a reversionary interest from a nonreversionary interest is easy if the interest was originally created during the transferor's lifetime, as in the examples above. When *G* carved out and conveyed a life estate to *A*, *G* retained what he did not transfer—a reversionary interest.

If *G* still owned the property in fee simple at his death, however, and devised a life estate in the property to *A* at that time, would the future interest be originally created in *G* or in a transferee? Common sense suggests that a dead transferor cannot retain anything. Yet the law views the situation differently. If *A*'s life estate was created in *G*'s will, the nature of the future interest depends on whether it also passed under G's will or whether it passed to G's heirs by intestacy.

Example 3.4: G's will devised land "to *A* for life." *G*'s will contained no residuary clause devising property not otherwise mentioned. Thus the rest of *G*'s property passed by intestacy to *G*'s sole heir, *B*.

B's interest is reversionary, because it did not pass to *B* by the same instrument as *A*'s interest.

Example 3.5: G's will devised land "to *A* for life" and devised the residue of his estate to *B*.

Most courts and authorities would say that *B*'s interest is nonreversionary, because it was created in *B* at the same time and by the same instrument (albeit not the same part of the instrument) as *A*'s life estate.

Example 3.6: G's will devised land "to A for life, and upon A's death, the land goes to B."

B's interest is clearly nonreversionary, because it was created in B at the same time and by the same part of the instrument (indeed, the same clause) as A's life estate.

§ 3.2 Reversionary Interests: Reversions, Reverters, Rights of Entry

If a future interest is reversionary, it is either a reversion, a possibility of reverter, or a right of entry.

Reversions are future interests retained by the transferor (or the transferor's successors in interest) when the transferor conveys an estate or estates of *less* quantum than the transferor had originally. The most common example is that of an owner of property in fee simple absolute who transfers out a particular estate (a possessory interest other than a fee simple interest).

Example 3.7: G conveyed land "to A for life."

G retained a reversionary interest, and that reversionary interest is called a reversion.

Example 3.8: G conveyed land "to *A* for life, then to *B* if *B* survives *A*."

G retained a reversionary interest, because *B*'s interest is subject to a condition precedent of survival (which might or might not be satisfied), and the conveyance does not provide for any other transferee to receive the property if *B* fails to survive. *G*'s reversionary interest is classified as a reversion, because the only vested estate in the sequence (*A*'s life estate) is of less quantum than *G*'s original fee simple absolute.

(The terms "condition precedent" and "vested" are explained in § 3.6.)

Possibilities of reverter are future interests retained by the transferor (or the transferor's successors in interest) when the transferor transfers out estates of the *same* quantum as the transferor had originally. The most common example is that of an owner of property in fee simple absolute who transfers out a fee simple determinable.

Example 3.9: G conveyed land "to *A* and his heirs so long as *A* does not allow liquor to be sold on the premises[, and upon *A*'s allowing liquor to be sold on the premises, the property is to revert to the grantor]."

G retained a reversionary interest, classified as a possibility of reverter.

The words contained in brackets in the preceding example are not necessary to create a possibility of reverter. Possibilities of reverter need not be expressly stated because, like reversions, they constitute an undisposed-of interest remaining in the transferor. See Simes & Smith on Future Interests § 286. In practice, however, it is common expressly to state the possibility of reverter, and a small minority of decisions has held (erroneously) that, without the bracketed words, *A* takes a fee simple absolute. See, e.g., *In re Copps Chapel Methodist Episcopal Church*, 120 Ohio St. 309, 166 N.E. 218 (1929).

A much rarer example of the possibility of reverter can be illustrated by a variation on Example 3.8.

Example 3.10: *G* conveyed land "to *A* for life, then to *B*, but if *B* fails to survive *A*, the property is to return to me."

G retained a reversionary interest, because *B*'s interest is subject to a condition of survival (which might or might not be satisfied), and the conveyance does not provide for any other transferee to receive the property if *B* fails to survive. *G*'s reversionary interest is classified as a possibility of reverter, not a remainder. The condition of survival is a condition subsequent, rendering *B*'s interest vested. (For elaboration, see Example 3.23.) *G* has thus conveyed out two vested interests, unlike in Example 3.8: *A*'s life estate and *B*'s remainder, which together are in effect a fee simple. The sum of these two vested interests yields an estate of the same quantum as *G* originally owned. Accordingly, G's retained interest is classified as a possibility of reverter. Restatement of Property § 154 cmt. e & illus. 2; Am. L. Prop. § 4.18.

Rights of entry[1] are future interests created in the transferor (or the transferor's successors in interest) when the transferor transfers an estate subject to a condition subsequent (i.e., subject to divestment). Whether the quantum is the same as or less than the transferor's original estate is unimportant. A

[1]Rights of entry go by other names: rights of re-entry, rights of entry for condition broken, powers of termination. The terms are interchangeable.

typical example is that of an owner of property in fee simple absolute who transfers out a fee simple subject to a condition subsequent and who expressly creates the right to re-enter and retake the premises if and when the condition is broken.

> *Example 3.11:* G conveyed land "to *A* and her heirs on condition that *A* not allow liquor to be sold on the premises[, but if *A* allows liquor to be sold on the premises, the grantor is to have the right to re-enter and take possession of the premises]."
>
> *G* retained (more accurately, created in himself) a reversionary interest, and that reversionary interest is called a right of entry.

The right of entry is different from other future interests in the following sense. The right of entry does not take effect in possession automatically when the condition is broken. If *A* allows liquor to be sold on the premises, *A*'s action merely gives *G* a right to elect to take a possessory interest if *G* so chooses. But this difference between rights of entry and other interests (for example, the possibility of reverter) may have little practical importance in the modern era. The early common-law rule was that a right of entry could be exercised only by a physical entry on the land. In most states today, however, the commencement of an action to regain possession satisfies the requirement of an election to divest the possessory estate, and the holder of a possibility of reverter often must institute a similar action in order to enforce his or her "automatic" interest. In addition, after the stipulated event has occurred, the time allowable under the law of many states for making an election under a right of entry is the same as that for bringing an action to enforce a possibility of reverter. The two possessory interests may thus be more in alignment than one would think.

There is another feature distinguishing rights of entry from reversions and possibilities of reverter. A right of entry is not the undisposed-of interest retained by the transferor when she transfers out other interests. Rather, it is a newly created future interest in the transferor. Does this mean that a right of entry must be expressly created? Theoretically, no. The transfer of a fee simple subject to a condition subsequent *by itself* causes a right of entry to arise in the grantor. Thus, in Example 3.11, omission of the bracketed portions of the disposition would not necessarily prevent *G* from having a right of entry. Simes and Smith on

Future Interests § 247. On the other hand, the law recognizes a strong constructional preference against forfeitures (in this example, against *A* forfeiting her present estate). It is possible, and perhaps even likely, that the omission of the bracketed portions would result in a court concluding that *G* had not intended to retain a right of entry. For further discussion see the next section.

§ 3.3 Ambiguous Language: Possibility of Reverter or Right of Entry?

The dispositive language in Examples 3.9 and 3.11 is unambiguous. Language granting *A* a fee simple determinable is followed by language describing a possibility of reverter; language granting *A* a fee simple subject to a condition subsequent is followed by language describing a right of entry.

In practice, unfortunately, the language of an actual disposition may be ambiguous. In such cases, courts often assert that forfeitures of present estates are disfavored in the law. Thus, a forfeiture will be avoided entirely if the language admits of some other construction and, if not, then at least the optional forfeiture incident to a right of entry will be preferred to the "automatic" forfeiture incident to a possibility of reverter. These constructional preferences gain strength as the amount of consideration paid by the grantee rises in relation to the value of a fee simple absolute in the land at the time of the grant. Nevertheless, these are tendencies only, and the result reached in any given case may be unpredictable. To avoid litigation, lawyers should be careful to use standard language, clearly coupling reverters with limitations, and rights of entry with conditions.

When litigation arises, cases of ambiguous language frequently fall into one of five categories.

First, the transfer may combine words of condition with a reverter clause ("to *A* and her heirs on condition that *A* never allow liquor to be sold, but if *A* allows liquor to be sold, the property is to revert to me"). Under the structure of estates, of course, a possibility of reverter can only follow a fee simple determinable, not a fee simple subject to a condition subsequent. Some courts resolve the contradiction by holding that the reverter language in the second clause means that the grantor intended to convey a fee simple determinable in the first clause. However, the Restatement of Property § 45 cmt m. and some other courts take the opposite view: the language of condition in the first clause is controlling and manifests an intention to retain only a right of entry. Still other courts reach the Restatement's conclusion by preferring the less drastic forfeiture of a right of entry over the "automatic" forfeiture of the possibility of reverter.

Second, the transfer may contain a statement of purpose plus a reverter clause (a transfer of land to a school district "to be used for school purposes and ceasing to be used for school purposes, it shall revert to the grantor"). Cases interpreting such clauses are split. Some hold that the unambiguous reverter language in the second clause means that the grantor intended to convey a fee simple determinable in the first clause. Others hold that the grantor retained only a right of entry; these latter cases often invoke the constructional preference against automatic forfeiture.

Third, the transfer may contain only a statement of purpose (a transfer of land to a school district "for school purposes"). The predominant result in such cases is to hold that the possessory estate is a fee simple absolute, with nothing retained by the grantor. See Restatement of Property § 45 cmt. o; *Town of Nahant v. United States*, 293 F. Supp. 1076 (D.Mass. 1968).

Fourth, the transfer may contain only words of limitation ("to the school district so long as used for school purposes"). The most likely result in such cases is to hold that a fee simple determinable was created in the transferee, leaving a possibility of reverter in the grantor.

Fifth and last, the transfer may contain only words of condition (to the grantee "on condition that the premises shall never be used as a tavern"). In the absence of an express right of entry, courts tend not to construe the estate as a fee simple subject to a condition subsequent. Instead, courts tend to construe the estate as a fee simple absolute: perhaps subject to a contractual obligation in favor of the grantor (a covenant restricting the use of the land); or perhaps subject to a trust obligation in favor of the grantor (a result especially likely when the grant was for a charitable purpose); or perhaps subject to an equitable charge or lien (a result likely if the condition requires the transferee to pay a sum of money to one or more third parties); or perhaps with no enforceable obligation at all. This last option renders the language in the grant merely an expression of the grantor's motives or purposes.

All of this discussion serves as a reminder of the drafting point made earlier: lawyers should be careful to use the language of estates and future interests clearly and correctly, so that courts do not have to guess the transferor's intention.

§ 3.4 Remainders

The one nonreversionary interest permitted at common law before the Statute of Uses (on which, see the next section) was the remainder.[2] A remainder is a future interest created in a transferee that becomes possessory if at all upon the natural termination of the preceding interest. The preceding interest (1) must have been created simultaneously with the creation of the future interest and (2) must be a particular estate. Recall that a particular estate is a term of art that denotes any possessory interest other than a fee simple interest.

> *Example 3.12: (1)* G transferred land "to *A* for life, and upon *A*'s death, to *B*."
>
> *(2)* G transferred land "to *A* for 10 years, and at the expiration thereof, to *B*."

---

[2]The term "remainder" was derived from the idea of an interest that "remained out" after the termination of a prior estate.

B has a remainder. (With respect to Variation (2), recall the discussion after Example 2.9.)

Example 3.13: (1) G transferred land "to *A* for life or until *A* remarries, and upon *A*'s death or remarriage, to *B*."

(2) G transferred land "to *A* for 10 years or until *A*'s remarriage, whichever sooner occurs, and upon the expiration of 10 years or *A*'s earlier remarriage, to *B*."

Technically, *B* has two interests, both remainders. But it is common to say simply that *B* has a remainder.

§ 3.5   The Statute of Uses and Executory Interests

The Statute of Uses, enacted in 1535 and effective in 1536, made possible a new nonreversionary future interest, called the executory interest. To understand the executory interest, you will need some brief historical background.

For much of its history, England had multiple, often overlapping systems of courts. Some courts were known as courts of common law, because their decisions created and enforced the common law. In addition, there was the Court of Chancery, headed by a senior royal official known as the Chancellor. The Chancellor was not bound by the rules of common law but instead was able to render decisions that took into account the justice or fairness of the parties' particular facts. The system of law administered by the Court of Chancery was known as equity.

Some property interests not recognized at common law were protected by the Court of Chancery. Consider the following example.

> *Example 3.14: G* transferred land "to *T* for *T* to hold, so that the property may be used by *A* for life, then by *B*."

From the perspective of the common law, the owner of the land was *T. T* had legal title, meaning title enforceable at common law. Where did that leave *A* and *B*? As far as the common law was concerned, *A* and *B* had no rights in the land. But *A* and *B* could go to the Court of Chancery, which recognized that the purpose of the transfer was to benefit *A* and *B*, not *T*. From the perspective of the Chancellor, *T* was merely a kind of trustee, holding the land for *A* and *B*. *T* might have the legal title, but it was *A* and *B* who had title in equity.

Why did *G* create this kind of transfer? The answer was (1) to avoid some then-existing forms of taxation, which would apply only to legal, not equitable, interests, and (2) to avoid medieval rules prohibiting the transfer of land by will.

The Statute of Uses was designed to stop this evasion. It stated in pertinent part: "[W]here any such person ... be seised ... in any lands ... to the use ... of any other person[,]... in every such case ... every such person ... that have ... any such use ... shall ... henceforth ... be seised ...." In other words, the statute transferred the legally recognized interests to the people who previously held only the use. Applying the Statute of Uses to Example 3.14: *A* holds a legal life estate, *B* holds a legal remainder, and *T* takes nothing.

The Statute of Uses had additional consequences. One of these was to permit the creation of a type of future interest that could not have been created at common law. Consider a variation on Example 3.11.

Example 3.15: G conveyed land "to *A* and her heirs on condition that *A* not allow liquor to be

sold on the premises, but if *A* allows liquor to
be sold on the premises, the land is to go to *B*."

In this example, *G* wants the sale of alcohol to
trigger, not a right of entry in himself, but instead
a transfer of the property to *B*. This result could not
be accomplished at common law, which permitted
defeasible fees to be followed only by reversionary
interests, not by nonreversionary interests. (Recall
§ 2.4.) After the Statute of Uses, however, *G* can
achieve the desired result, as illustrated in the
following example.

Example 3.16: *G* conveyed land "to *T* for the
use of *A* and her heirs on condition that *A* not
allow liquor to be sold on the premises, but if *A*
allows liquor to be sold on the premises, the
property is to be for the use of *B*."

The Statute of Uses created legally-recognized
interests in *A* and *B*. Over time, these interests
became accepted even without the intermediate
transfer to *T*. Each of the interests has a name: *B*'s
future interest is called an *executory interest*; *A*'s
present estate is called a *fee simple subject to an
executory limitation*.

The Statute of Uses also had the effect of permitting nonreversionary interests to follow the fee simple determinable. These interests are also called executory interests.

Example 3.17: G transferred land "to *A* and her heirs so long as *A* does not allow liquor to be sold on the premises, and upon *A*'s allowing liquor to be sold on the premises, to *B*."

After the Statute of Uses, *B* has an executory interest.

One can also create executory interests following estates less than fee simple.

Example 3.18: (1) G transferred land "to *A* for life, and upon *A*'s death, to *B*; but if *A* remarries, the land goes to *B* immediately."

(2) G transferred land "to *A* for 10 years, and at the expiration thereof, to *B*; but if during the 10-year period *A* remarries, the land goes to *B* immediately."

B has both an executory interest and a remainder. The executory interest takes effect in possession if *A* remarries. The remainder takes effect in possession if *A* does not remarry. (On Variation (2), recall the discussion after

Example 2.9.)

Executory interests are sometimes divided into two categories—springing and shifting. *Shifting* executory interests potentially divest an interest conferred by the grantor on a transferee. *Springing* executory interests potentially divest an interest retained by the grantor.

> *Example 3.19: (1) G* transferred land "to *A* and his heirs, but if *A* allows liquor to be sold on the premises, to *B*."
>
> *(2) G* transferred land "to *B* and her heirs, to take effect in possession on *B*'s future marriage."
>
> *B*'s executory interest is *shifting* in Variation (1) and *springing* in Variation (2).

§ 3.6 Classification in Terms of Vesting

Future interests are subject to a further level of classification—classification in terms of vesting. There are four categories here: indefeasibly vested, vested subject to (complete) defeasance, vested subject to open (partial defeasance), and contingent (nonvested).

An *indefeasibly vested* future interest is one that is not subject to any conditions or limitations. In other words, the future interest must be certain to become a possessory fee simple absolute at some time in the future. Only remainders and reversions can be indefeasibly vested.

> *Example 3.20:* G transferred land "to *A* for life, remainder to *B*."

B's remainder is indefeasibly vested. It is certain to become possessory because *A* is bound to die. When *A* dies, *B*'s remainder will become a possessory fee simple absolute.

Note in this example that *B* might not be alive when *A* dies. Except as otherwise provided by statute, *B*'s interest is not subject to a condition of survival of *A*. Therefore, the possibility of *B*'s death before *A*'s death has no bearing on the classification of *B*'s interest. If *B* dies before *A*, *B*'s indefeasibly vested remainder will pass at *B*'s death to *B*'s successors in interest—her devisees or, if she dies intestate, her heirs.

> *Example 3.21:* G conveyed land "to *A* for life."

G's reversion is indefeasibly vested. The

comments made in the previous example regarding *B*'s remainder apply to *G*'s reversion in this example.

Example 3.22: G conveyed land "to *A* for life, remainder to *B* for 10 years."

G's reversion is indefeasibly vested. It is certain to become possessory 10 years after *A*'s death, and will at that time become a fee simple absolute.

B's remainder is not indefeasibly vested. Although it is certain to become possessory upon *A*'s death (a certain event), it will not become a fee simple absolute then. *B*'s remainder is vested subject to defeasance after 10 years. The comments made in Example 3.20 regarding survival apply equally here.

A future interest that is *vested subject to defeasance* is one that is subject to one or more conditions subsequent or to one or more limitations. The precise terminology to be used will depend on whether the interest is subject to conditions subsequent, on the one hand, or to limitations, on the other hand. (Recall the definitions of these terms in § 2.4.)

If the future interest is subject to one or more *conditions subsequent*, it is called *vested subject to divestment*. Only remainders and reversions can be vested subject to divestment. Note, however, that there is an important difference between remainders and reversions. Remainders are vested subject to divestment only when they are subject to a condition subsequent. (As we shall shortly see, remainders subject to a condition precedent are contingent.) In contrast, reversions are vested subject to divestment whenever they are subject to a condition, regardless of whether the condition is precedent or subsequent. The reason for this difference is that, by definition, reversions can never be contingent. *Reversions are always vested.*

Example 3.23: G transferred land "to *A* for life, remainder to *B*, but if *B* fails to survive *A*, to *C*."

B's remainder is vested subject to divestment because the condition of survival attached to her remainder is stated in condition subsequent form—"to *B*, but if."

C's executory interest is subject to the condition that *B* not survive *A*. From *C*'s perspective, the condition is stated in the form of a condition precedent—"if...to *C*." Thus, *C*'s executory interest is contingent.

Example 3.24: G conveyed land "to A for life, remainder to B if B survives A, but if not, to return to me."

B's remainder is subject to a condition of survival of A, but this time the condition is stated in the form of a condition precedent—"to B if." B's remainder is therefore contingent, not vested subject to divestment.

G's reversion is subject to the condition that B not survive A. From G's perspective, the condition is a condition precedent—"if...to return to me." This indicates that G's reversion should be classified as contingent. However, the rule that reversions are always vested overrides all other rules. Thus, G's reversion is vested subject to divestment.

Example 3.25: G conveyed land "to A for life, remainder to B if B survives A, but if not, to C."

B's remainder is subject to a condition of survival of A that is stated in the form of a condition precedent—"to B if." B's remainder is therefore contingent.

C's remainder is subject to the condition that

B not survive *A*. The condition is stated in the form of a condition precedent ("if [*B* does not survive *A*], to *C*") and, therefore, *C*'s remainder is contingent.

G retained a technical reversion. (There is always a reversion when a particular estate is followed by contingent remainders. In a case such as this example, the contingencies stated with respect to the interests of *B* and *C* exhaust all the possibilities; hence, the reversion is said to be merely "technical."[3]) The reversion is vested subject to divestment because reversions are always vested rather than contingent.

The preceding examples—especially Examples 3.23 and 3.25—reveal that the distinction between a vested remainder subject to divestment and a contingent remainder rests on form, not substance. In both examples, *G* wants to subject *B*'s possession to the requirement that *B* outlive *A*. The only difference is the form of the requirement: a condition subsequent in Example 3.23 versus a condition precedent in Example 3.25. The

---

[3]The presence of a technical reversion matters only in jurisdictions retaining the rule of the destructibility of contingent remainders, discussed in § 6.1.

distinction is artificial because the requirement can be stated either way. Yet the distinction is important to learn because substantive legal consequences do flow from the classification, as we shall see in Chapters 4-6.

A future interest that is subject to one or more limitations (recall the definition of this word: such interests expire naturally or by their own terms, e.g., an interest for life) is called *vested subject to limitational defeasance*. Only remainders and reversions can be vested subject to limitational defeasance.

>*Example 3.26:* G transferred land "to *A* for life, then to *B* for life, then to *C*."
>
>*B*'s remainder is vested subject to limitational defeasance. It is sometimes referred to simply as a vested remainder for life. Note that *B* must survive *A* for his interest to become possessory. This implicit requirement of survival is not regarded as a "condition" of survival.
>
>*C*'s interest is a remainder because *B*'s interest is subject to a limitation and because it is an estate less than a fee simple. It is an indefeasibly vested remainder because it is subject to no condition or limitation.

Example 3.27: G conveyed land "to A for life, then to return to me for life, then to C."

This is the same as the previous example, except that the future interest subject to limitational defeasance is a reversion in G rather than a remainder in B.

Example 3.28: G transferred land "to A for life, then to B for 10 years, then to C."

B's remainder is vested subject to limitational defeasance. In this case, the time of B's death is irrelevant. If B dies while A is still alive, B's remainder will pass to her devisee or if she died intestate to her heirs. If B dies after A's death but before the 10th anniversary thereof, the remaining portion of B's 10-year term will pass to her devisee or if she died intestate to her heirs.

A future interest—typically a remainder—is *vested subject to open* when it is subject to no conditions precedent and when it is in favor of a class that contains at least one living member and that is still "open," i.e., where it is possible for additional persons to become class members (typically through birth or adoption). (On the concept of a class gift, see § 5.8). Other and older labels for this type of interest are *vested subject to partial divestmen*t or *vested in quality but not in quantity*. These terms are descriptive of the phenomenon that each time a new member is added to the class the shares of the existing class members are reduced (partially divested). Whichever label is used, it is important to note that the existing class members are the ones who are regarded as having a remainder vested subject to open. The interests of the unborn or unadopted class members are contingent on being born or adopted. They are executory interests because upon birth or adoption they partially divest the interests or shares of the living class members.

Example 3.29: G transferred land "to *A* for life, remainder to his children." When the transfer was made, *A* had two children, *X* and *Y*. Later a third child, *Z*, was born.

At the time of the transfer, *X* has a vested remainder subject to open in an undivided half of the property; *Y* has a vested remainder subject to open in the other undivided half; the unborn children have executory interests. Upon *Z*'s birth, *Z*'s executory interest becomes a vested remainder subject to open in an undivided third of the property, and X's and Y's interests are reduced (or partially divested) to vested remainders subject to open in an undivided third.

The executory interest, the only other nonreversionary future interest, can be in favor of a class that is subject to open, but the executory interest itself cannot be called vested subject to open because executory interests are, almost by definition, contingent. (See footnote 5.)

A future interest is *contingent* (nonvested)[4] if it is subject to a condition precedent. A condition precedent may be explicit or implicit. An explicit condition precedent exists where the language of the disposition declares that the interest is to become possessory *if* some event occurs. Implicit conditions precedent exist when the future interest is in favor of unborn or unascertained persons.

Remainders can be contingent but need not be.

_____

[4] The traditional term is *contingent*, but some authorities use the term *nonvested*.

Executory interests are nearly always contingent.[5] Reversions cannot be contingent but possibilities of reverter and rights of entry are regarded as contingent for most purposes (although not for the Rule Against Perpetuities).[6]

---

[5]The typical executory interest is subject to a condition precedent and is classified as contingent. In rare cases, an executory interest is created that is unconditional. An example would be if *G* conveyed land "to *B* and his heirs, to take effect in possession 25 years from now." Another example would be if *G* conveyed land "to *B* and his heirs, to take effect in possession at my death." It is assumed in each case that the possessory interest retained by *G* is a fee simple interest, not a term of 25 years or a life estate. This means that *B*'s future interest cannot be a remainder and, therefore, must be an executory interest. If it were a remainder, it would be classified as indefeasibly vested. The courts have been reluctant to call this type of an executory interest vested. Its classification has been perplexing because it is an executory interest. Nevertheless, it is generally assumed that, like vested interests in general, this type of an executory interest is not subject to the Rule Against Perpetuities.

[6]Although possibilities of reverter and rights of entry are classified as contingent, they are not subject to the Rule Against Perpetuities. This anomaly was noted by Professor John Chipman Gray in his classic treatise. Gray agreed that possibilities of reverter were, and should be, exempt from the Rule, and so he maintained that there was "no practical object" in labeling them as contingent. Gray on Perpetuities § 113.3. Conversely, Gray argued that rights of entry, as truly continent interests, should be subject to the Rule. *Id*. at § 310.

Example 3.30: G conveyed land "to A for life, remainder to B if B survives A."

B's remainder is contingent because the condition of surviving A is stated in the form of a condition precedent—"to B if."

G's reversion appears to be subject to the condition precedent that B not survive A, but G's reversion is vested subject to divestment because of the rule that reversions are always vested. This means that B's remainder in this situation acts like an executory interest because it potentially divests G's reversion. Nevertheless, it is a remainder because its predominant feature is that it takes effect in possession, if at all, on the natural termination of A's life estate.

Example 3.31: G transferred land "to A for life, remainder to A's children." When the transfer was made, A had no children.

A's unborn children have contingent remainders. Their remainders, unlike B's remainder in the previous example, are implicitly contingent on being born or adopted, but are not contingent on surviving A.

Example 3.32: G transferred land "to A for life, remainder to A's heirs."

The remainder in favor of A's heirs is contingent because it is in favor of unascertained persons. The persons who are A's heirs cannot be ascertained until A's death.

Nevertheless, any person who would be an heir of A if A were to die immediately is called an heir apparent or an heir expectant. The heirs expectant are regarded as having contingent remainders during A's lifetime rather than mere expectancies. Thus it is sometimes said that they take by purchase rather than by succession or descent. Their remainders are implicitly contingent on their actually becoming A's heirs when A dies.

Example 3.33: G transferred land "to A for life, remainder to B, but if B fails to survive A, to C."

The condition that B survive A is a condition subsequent as to B's remainder ("to B, but if"), making it vested subject to divestment. C's executory interest is contingent, for it is subject to the condition precedent that B not survive A.

Example 3.34: (1) G transferred land "to *A* and her heirs on condition that *A* never allow liquor to be sold on the premises, but if *A* allows liquor to be sold on the premises, the property is to go to *B*."

(2) G transferred land "to *A* and her heirs for as long as *A* never allows liquor to be sold on the premises, and upon *A*'s allowing liquor to be sold on the premises, the property is to go to *B*."

B's executory interest is subject to the condition that *A* allow liquor to be sold on the premises. In both Variations, the condition is in condition precedent form and, therefore, *B*'s executory interest is contingent.

Example 3.35: (1) G conveyed land "to *A* and his heirs on condition that *A* never allow liquor to be sold on the premises, but if *A* allows liquor to be sold on the premises, the grantor shall have the right to re-enter and take possession of the premises."

(2) G conveyed land "to *A* and his heirs for as long as *A* never allows liquor to be sold on the premises, and upon *A*'s allowing liquor to be sold on the premises, the premises are to revert to the grantor."

G's right of entry in Variation (1) and *G*'s possibility of reverter in Variation (2) would appear to be subject to the condition precedent that *A* allow liquor to be sold on the premises. Most authorities do in fact classify these interests as contingent.

§ 3.7   Future Interests in Sets: Rules of Thumb

When a *defeasible fee simple* is followed by more than one nonreversionary future interest, only one of which can become possessory, all the future interests are executory interests, for a remainder cannot follow a fee simple estate. (Recall § 3.4.)

> *Example 3.36:* *G* transferred land "to *A* and his heirs, but if *A* allows liquor to be sold on the land, to *B* if *B* is then living, and if *B* is not then living, to *C*."
>
> *B* and *C* have executory interests.

When a particular estate (a life estate or term of years) is followed by more than one nonreversionary future interest, the first future interest will always be a remainder. The other or subsequent future interest(s), however, may be either remainders or executory interests. In determining which they are, the following rules apply:

Rule 1: If the first future interest is a contingent remainder, the other nonreversionary future interests will also be contingent remainders.

Rule 2: If the first future interest is a vested remainder subject to divestment, the other nonreversionary future interests will be executory interests.

The rules are illustrated in the following examples.

Example 3.37: G transferred land "to A for life, remainder to B if B survives A, but if not, to C."

Because B has a contingent remainder, C has a contingent remainder. For convenience, B's and C's interests are known as *alternative contingent remainders*.

Example 3.38: G transferred land "to A for life, remainder to B, but if B fails to survive A, to *C*."

Because *B*'s remainder is vested subject to divestment, *C* has an executory interest.

§ 3.8 Permissible Changes in Classification Due to Subsequent Events

We learned in § 3.1 that reversionary interests do not become nonreversionary by virtue of a post-creation transfer to a transferee. Likewise, nonreversionary interests do not become reversionary by virtue of a post-creation transfer to the transferor.

Some changes in classification due to post-creation events are permissible, however. Specifically, executory interests can become remainders, contingent remainders can become vested remainders, and (unless the rule of the destructibility of contingent remainders applies, on which see § 6.1) remainders can become executory interests. Consider the following examples.

Example 3.39: *G* transferred land "to *A* for life, remainder to *B*, but if *B* fails to survive *A*, to *C*." *B* predeceases *A*.

At creation, *B*'s interest is a vested remainder subject to divestment and *C*'s interest is an executory interest.

At *B*'s death, *B*'s vested remainder is divested and *C*'s executory interest becomes an indefeasibly vested remainder. This points to the misleading nature of a statement that is unfortunately often repeated by courts: that an executory interest cannot vest until it vests in possession. In fact, an executory interest can vest before becoming possessory by changing into a remainder.

Example 3.40: *G* transferred land "to *A* for life, remainder to *B* if *B* survives *A*, but if not, to *C*." *B* predeceases *A*.

At creation, *B*'s and *C*'s interests are alternative contingent remainders. At *B*'s death, *B*'s contingent remainder is defeated, *G*'s technical reversion is divested, and *C*'s contingent remainder becomes an indefeasibly vested remainder.

Example 3.41: *G* transferred land "to *A* for life, remainder to *B* if *B* lives to age 21." The destructibility rule has been abolished by statute in the jurisdiction.

If *B* reaches 21 while *A* is alive, *B*'s contingent remainder becomes indefeasibly vested, and G's reversion is divested.

If B is younger than 21 when A dies, B's contingent remainder becomes an executory interest. G's reversion takes effect in possession upon A's death as a fee simple subject to defeasance in favor of B if and when B later reaches 21.

Example 3.42: G transferred land "to A for life, remainder to A's children, but if none of A's children survives A, to B." When the transfer was made, A had no children. Later a child, X, was born to A. Thereafter, but still during A's lifetime, X died. The destructibility rule has been abolished by statute in the jurisdiction.

At creation, A's unborn children have contingent remainders, because they are subject to the implicit condition precedent of being born to or adopted by A. B has an alternative contingent remainder, and G has a technical reversion.

When X is born, X takes a vested remainder subject to divestment and subject to open. B's interest and the interests of A's unborn children change into executory interests, and G's technical reversion is divested.

When *X* dies, *B*'s interests and the interests of *A*'s unborn children do not change back into alternative contingent remainders because *X* does not lose his interest. *X*'s interest, which remains subject to complete divestment only if *A* leaves *no* surviving children and to partial divestment if *A* has additional children, passes through *X*'s estate to *X*'s successors in interest.

§ 3.9   Future Interests Belonging to More Than One Category

Often a future interest will be subject to open but the phrase "subject to open" will not appear in its classification because it is contingent. This does not mean that the interest is not actually subject to open; it merely means that the fact is not expressed.

Example 3.43: *G* transferred land "to *A* for life, remainder to *A*'s children who survive *A*; but if none survives *A*, to *B*."

The remainders in *A*'s children are contingent. They are also subject to open, but recognition of this fact by using the phrase "contingent subject to open" is not done.

§ 3.10 Failure of a Nonreversionary Future Interest

A nonreversionary future interest can fail for any variety of reasons. The beneficiary might predecease the testator or predecease a subsequent time to which survival is required by the terms of the disposition; the future interest might be disclaimed; it might violate the Rule Against Perpetuities (on which see Chapter 5); and so on.

The question addressed in this section is the effect of the failure of an executory interest following a fee simple estate. On this point, courts have reached different results depending on whether the estate is a fee simple determinable or a fee simple subject to a condition subsequent. Consider the following examples.

Example 3.44: G transferred land "to X-Church so long as the land is used for church purposes, and if church use ever ceases, to *B*." X-Church has a fee simple determinable, and *B* has an executory interest.

Example 3.45: G transferred land "to X-Church on condition that the land is used for church purposes, and if church use ever ceases, to *B*." X-Church has a fee simple subject to a condition subsequent, and *B* has an executory interest.

In each of these two examples, *B*'s executory interest violates the Rule Against Perpetuities and is therefore invalid. The question is: what is the effect of the invalidity? According to the case law, the church's interest in Example 3.44 remains a fee simple determinable with a possibility of reverter in *G*, whereas the church's interest in Example 3.45 becomes a fee simple absolute. *First Universalist Soc'y of North Adams v. Boland*, 155 Mass. 171, 29 N.E. 524 (1892); *Proprietors of the Church in Brattle Square v. Grant*, 69 Mass. 142 (1855). A different view appears in the Restatement 2d of Property § 1.5 cmts. b & c, which suggest that the church's interest in both instances should be a fee simple absolute.

§ 3.11   The Law Favors the Vesting of Estates

The law traditionally prefers vested interests to contingent ones. As was colorfully stated in *Roberts v. Roberts*, 2 Bulstrode 123, 80 Eng. Rep. 1002 (K.B. 1613), "the law always delights in the vesting of estates, and contingencies are odious in the law, and are the causes of troubles, and vesting and settling of estates, the cause of repose and certainty."

The source of the preference for vested interests is complex, but it is commonly claimed that it arose from the desire to avoid certain common-law rules, such as the destructibility rule and the Rule Against Perpetuities, to promote alienability, to promote completeness of the disposition, and to promote equality of distribution among different lines of descent.

In general, it can be said that courts will construe a provision as not imposing a condition precedent if they can do so without contradicting the express language of the instrument, i.e., where there is sufficient ambiguity in the language to permit what might be called an even choice.

An illustration of this preference can be seen with respect to the remainder for life ("to *A* for life, then to *B* for life, then to *C*"). *B*'s remainder for life could in theory have been classified as contingent upon surviving *A*. In fact, remainders for life are held to become vested at the birth of the taker (here, *B*'s birth) and are vested subject to limitational defeasance (*B*'s eventual and certain death). This classification obtains even where survivorship is expressly phrased as a condition precedent, as in the following example.

Example 3.46: G transferred land "to A for life, remainder to B for life if B survives A."

Most courts ignore the express condition of survivorship as mere surplusage and classify B's remainder as vested, not contingent.

Another illustration of the preference for vested interests can be seen with respect to remainders subject to a power. (We shall discuss powers in Part IV.) Frequently someone will be given a power to divert the property to someone other than the beneficiary of the remainder interest. This kind of condition is not considered a condition precedent.

Example 3.47: G transferred land "to A for life, remainder to the persons A shall by will appoint, and in default of appointment, to B."

B's remainder is vested subject to divestment by the exercise of the power by A.

A similar result is reached in cases involving a remainder subject to a charge or lien, as in the following example.

Example 3.48: G transferred land "to A for life, remainder B if B pays C $5,000 within in one year of A's death."

By the prevailing view, B takes the land at A's death subject to a charge or lien in favor of C. If B does not pay the $5,000 to C within a reasonable time, C can enforce the charge or lien in that amount against the land. Had the court instead held that B's remainder was contingent on paying the money, B would have lost the land and C would not have received the money; neither of these results accomplishes G's objective.

CHAPTER 4

ALIENABILITY OF FUTURE INTERESTS

The discussion of the alienation of future interests must be divided into transfers at death (by will or by intestacy) and transfers during lifetime (inter vivos).

§ 4.1   Transferability at Death: Intestacy and Will

Future interests are generally *descendible*, meaning capable of passing by intestacy. At one time, the course of descent for future interests was different from that of possessory estates. The details need not trouble us here; they are described in Simes & Smith on Future Interests § 1882; Am. L. Prop. § 4.73. The divergent course of descent for future interests was abolished by statute in England in 1897, and today in the United States reversions, remainders, and executory interests descend according to the same rules and in the same proportions as possessory estates. Everywhere except South Carolina, possibilities of reverter and rights of entry also descend according to the same rules applicable to possessory estates. In South Carolina, possibilities of reverter and rights of entry do not descend. See *Purvis v. McElveen*, 234 S.C. 94, 106 S.E.2d 913 (1959).

Future interests are also generally *devisable*, meaning capable of passing by will. This is true in all U.S. states for reversions, remainders, and executory interests, and in most states for possibilities of reverter and rights of entry. See Simes & Smith on Future Interests § 1903.

There is an obvious exception to the above rules for interests conditioned upon the beneficiary's survival. A future interest is descendible and devisable only if the beneficiary's death does not extinguish the interest. Consider the following example.

Example 4.1: G transferred land "to A for life, remainder to B, but if B fails to survive A, to C." C died, then B, then A.

C's executory interest is not contingent on C's survival. Thus, C's executory interest is descendible and devisable.

B's remainder was vested subject to divestment if *B* failed to survive *A*. On these facts, *B* did die before *A*, hence the remainder was extinguished at *B*'s death.

§ 4.2 Voluntary Transfer During Life

Reversions and vested remainders have long been alienable inter vivos. Contingent remainders were traditionally considered by the common law as inalienable inter vivos on the ground that they were too speculative; they were mere possibilities of receiving an interest in the future, rather than property interests in their own right. When executory interests were recognized, they were regarded as sufficiently analogous to contingent remainders to warrant the same treatment.

Despite this inalienability rule, holders of these contingent interests in England still found three ways to make transfers: contracts were enforceable if adequate consideration had been received by the transferor; deeds were enforceable if the deed contained a covenant of warranty, thereby estopping the transferor from challenging the transferee's title; and releases were enforceable if the release was in favor of the person whose future interest would be defeated if the released interest were to vest. With these exceptions, the common-law rule boiled down to this: purported transfers for inadequate consideration by quitclaim deed to someone other than a person in whose favor the interest could have been released were ineffective.

Today, most U.S. states have abolished the inalienability rule by statute or judicial decision, thus making contingent remainders and executory interests transferable inter vivos. A few states follow the common-law rule of inalienability while also recognizing the three forms of transfer that were available in England. A few other states make alienability depend upon the type of contingency: interests contingent on an event (surviving the life tenant, for example) are alienable, but interests contingent as to person (for instance, class gifts, in which some beneficiaries may be unborn or unascertained) are not.

Example 4.2: G transferred land "to *A* for life, remainder to *B* if *B* survives *A*; if not, to *B*'s heirs."

B's remainder is contingent as to event, and under this rule would be alienable. The remainder in *B*'s heirs, however, is contingent as to person and would be inalienable.

But these are minority positions. Most U.S. states treat contingent remainders and executory interests as fully transferable.

There is an important sense, however, in which contingent interests are impossible to alienate, namely when there is no one who can consent to the alienation. Consider a transfer "to *A* for life, remainder to *A*'s children." If *A* has living children, their remainder interests can be alienated either by themselves if they possess legal capacity or, if not, by their legal guardian. But if *A* is childless, there may be no one—not even *A*—who can consent to the alienation. Guardians in the traditional sense can be appointed only for living persons. Many jurisdictions authorize a specially appointed fiduciary called a guardian ad litem to represent the interests of unborn or unascertained beneficiaries in litigation, but the law seldom authorizes this fiduciary to join in a transfer of property. For a statute authorizing such consent, see UTC § 305.

With respect to possibilities of reverter and rights of entry, U.S. jurisdictions are divided. Some permit alienation of one or both; others do not. The alienability of possibilities of reverter, but not of unexercised rights of entry, is advocated by the Restatement of Property §§ 159, 160.

§ 4.3   Involuntary Transfer: Creditors' Rights

State statutes provide creditors with the right to impound their debtors' assets prior to judgment and the right after judgment to subject their assets to sale. These statutes purport to specify the types of assets that are subject to these procedures, but the statutory language is usually so general that courts must decide whether the debtor's future interests can be affected.

The general principle followed by the courts under these statutes is that if the future interest is voluntarily alienable, it is also subject to the claims of creditors. Indefeasibly vested remainders and reversions, since they are voluntarily alienable, are automatically available to creditors in the satisfaction of their claims. The same is true of remainders and reversions that are vested subject to defeasance.

Contingent remainders and executory interests are not subject to the claims of creditors in the minority of states in which they are not voluntarily alienable. The fact that the English methods of conveyance (the equitable contract to convey, the estoppel by deed, and the release) are available does not change the result. In the vast majority of states, these interests can be alienated, and the courts rather routinely hold such interests subject to creditors' claims. See Restatement of Property §§ 166, 167.

There is a potential problem with selling future interests to satisfy creditors: the sale of a future interest that is subject to conditions will undoubtedly bring a low purchase price. In such an event, the sale would not substantially benefit the creditor and might do serious harm to the debtor by depriving him or her of the future possibility of gaining property of much higher value. The winner in such situations is neither the debtor nor the creditor but the purchaser at the sale. (There is, of course, the chance that the purchaser may be the creditor.) In a tiny handful of cases, courts have responded to this problematic scenario by exercising their equitable powers to depart from the general rule on creditors' rights in cases involving equitable future interests, meaning future interests in trust. In at least one case, the court held that the future interest was subject to contingencies so remote that the creditor should simply be denied access to it. *Clarke v. Fay*, 205 Mass. 228, 91 N.E. 328 (1910). In another case, the court permitted access but refused to order an immediate sale of the interest, imposing instead a lien on the future interest until the contingencies were satisfied, if ever. *Meyer v. Reif*, 217 Wis. 11, 258 N.W. 391(1935). We find this last solution—a lien—a promising alternative to the immediate sale. It is worth considering for all equitable future interests, even ones not subject to remote contingencies. No future interest, even one indefeasibly vested, would bring a sale price equal to the value of immediate possession of the trust fund, hence the attractiveness of a lien rather than an immediate judgment sale.

So far we have been speaking of a creditor's rights under state law during the debtor's lifetime. This leaves two topics to be addressed. First, the creditor's rights under state law after the debtor's death. Second, a creditor's rights under federal bankruptcy law.

When the owner of a future interest dies, the interest might be transmissible by will even if it was not alienable inter vivos. It may be argued that the decedent's creditors should be satisfied from such assets. There appears to be little law on the subject. Some state statutes governing the payment of claims against decedents' estates answer the matter by equating the creditor's rights to the property that the decedent could have alienated inter vivos. Text writers and the Restatement of Property § 169 indicate that the same result will probably be reached in situations where the controlling statute is not explicit.

In federal bankruptcy proceedings, the rights of creditors are far-reaching. Federal law treats "all legal or equitable [property] interests of the debtor" as part of the bankrupt's estate "notwithstanding any provision in ... nonbankruptcy law ... that restricts ... transfer of such interest by the debtor ...." 11 U.S.C. § 541. This language is broad enough to include all classifications of future interests, even those immune from creditors under state law.

CHAPTER 5

THE RULE AGAINST PERPETUITIES

§ 5.1   Introduction

The Rule Against Perpetuities was originally designed to prevent the dead hand from indirectly curtailing the alienability of property for too long a period—in perpetuity. The indirect curtailment of alienability was said to arise from attaching contingencies to future interests in property.

A rule that developed, step by step over time, into the rule known today as the Rule Against Perpetuities was initiated in the much-celebrated *Duke of Norfolk's Case*, 3 Ch. Cas. 1, 22 Eng. Rep. 931 (Ch. 1682). The so-called modern Rule Against Perpetuities was formulated by Professor John Chipman Gray in the second edition of his book, The Rule Against Perpetuities (2d ed. 1906). Professor Gray's book solidified the Rule Against Perpetuities, stunting its further evolution throughout much of the twentieth century. But the Rule Against Perpetuities is again undergoing change. These changes are mainly in the form of perpetuity-reform legislation, though there have also been some developments at common law. Among the most important reforms are the promulgation of the Uniform Statutory Rule Against Perpetuities, discussed in § 5.14, and the emergence of the dynasty trust, discussed in § 5.16.

§ 5.2   Statement of the Rule at Common Law

The classic statement of the Rule Against Perpetuities was formulated by Professor John

Chipman Gray in the second edition of his book, The Rule Against Perpetuities (2d ed. 1906):

> *No [nonvested property] interest is good unless it must vest, if at all, not later than 21 years after some life in being at the creation of the interest.*

Nothing resembling this mechanically precise "rule" was stated by the judge in the *Duke of Norfolk's Case*, the Lord Chancellor, the First Earl of Nottingham. His pronouncements about prohibiting perpetuities appear to be mere musings:

> But what Time? And where are the Bounds of that Contingency? You may limit, it seems, upon a Contingency to happen in a Life: What if it be limited, if such a one die without Issue within twenty-one Years, or 100 Years, or while Westminster-Hall stands? Where will you stop, if you do not stop here? I will tell you where I will stop: I will stop wherever any visible Inconvenience doth appear;....

Gradually, over the 150 or so years following the *Duke of Norfolk's Case*, the pronouncement that a contingency limited to "happen in a Life" was valid, but beyond that, an invalidity would arise "wherever any visible Inconvenience doth appear," grew step by step into the Rule Against Perpetuities stated by Professor Gray.

§ 5.3   Interests Subject to the Rule

The Rule Against Perpetuities applies to future interests in property, whether legal or equitable, but only if they are contingent (nonvested). Classification of the interests in a disposition is, therefore, a preliminary but crucial step to solving perpetuity questions. Specifically, the Rule applies to contingent remainders and to executory interests, both of which are nonvested future interests. The Rule does not apply to vested remainders, not even to those that are vested subject to defeasance; nor does the Rule apply to reversions, which are always vested. The other two reversionary future interests—possibilities of reverter and rights of entry—are also considered exempt from the Rule Against Perpetuities.[1]

---

[1] See § 3.6 note 6. Some states have statutes that terminate possibilities of reverter and rights of entry after a certain period of time. The statutes vary in detail, but they generally state that these interests cease to exist if the event upon which they are predicated has not occurred within a certain period

Class gifts (such as a transfer to "children" or "descendants"; see § 5.8) are also subject to the Rule, and in fact are treated specially. The early English decision of *Leake v. Robinson*, 2 Mer. 363, 35 Eng. Rep. 979 (Ch. 1817), laid down the proposition that *if the interest of any potential class member might vest too remotely, the entire class gift is invalid.* This is the so-called all-or-nothing rule, by which it is meant that a class gift is either completely valid or completely invalid. It is not permissible to treat the interest of each class member separately and say that some class members have valid interests and other class members have invalid interests.

§ 5.4   The "Perpetuity Period"

The common-law perpetuity period is defined as a life in being plus 21 years. The period can be extended by one or more periods of gestation, *but only when an actual pregnancy makes the extension necessary.*

The life in being, often called the *measuring life*, must be the life of a person "in being at the

of time—ranging from thirty to fifty years. The effect of their termination is to render the possessory estate absolute.

creation of the interest." This means that the person whose life is the measuring life must be alive or in gestation when the perpetuity period begins to run. The measuring life must also be a human life—the life of a corporation, an animal, or a plant cannot be used. But there are no further restrictions. Theoretically, anyone in the world who was alive or in gestation when the interest was created can be the measuring life. As a practical matter, though, it is not that complex, as we shall see, when one gets down to identifying the measuring life in actual cases.

As noted above, a child in gestation at the commencement of the perpetuity period can be a measuring life because the child is considered then to be "in being." So also the perpetuity period is expandable at the end to account for an actual period of gestation, if necessary.

§ 5.5   The Requirement of Initial Certainty

Implicit in Professor Gray's formulation is the *requirement of initial certainty*, which is that a contingent future interest is invalid if, at the creation of the interest, there exists any possible chain of events that might subsequently arise that would allow the interest to remain contingent beyond a life in being plus 21 years. The life in being is traditionally called the "measuring life."

Only valid dispositions produce a particular life who has the requisite causal connection and is identified as the so-called measuring life. An invalid interest is invalid because there is *no* measuring life that makes it valid—not because it might remain contingent beyond 21 years after the death of an identifiable measuring life. This is what is meant when it is said that invalidity under the common-law Rule depends upon the existence, as of the interest's creation, of an invalidating chain of possible post-creation events. *The search for a "measuring life," therefore, turns out in reality to be a search for a "validating life."*

The requirement of initial certainty is a mechanism for testing the validity of an interest *in advance* of its actual vesting or termination. With the decision made in advance, the common law has no need to mark off a "perpetuity period" in the case of invalid interests. Here is why: A "perpetuity period" would be necessary only if actual post-creation events were to be taken into account. But the common-law Rule does not permit post-creation events to be considered.

§ 5.6   How to Search for a Validating Life

The Official Comment to § 1 of the Uniform Rule sets forth the following guidance for solving a perpetuities problem:

> The process for determining whether a validating life exists is to postulate the death of each individual connected in some way to the transaction, and ask the question: Is there with respect to this individual an invalidating chain of possible [post-creation] events? If one individual can be found for whom the answer is No, that individual can serve as the validating life. As to that individual there will be the requisite causal connection between his or her death and the questioned interest's vesting or terminating no later than 21 years thereafter.

Note that the converse is also true: If no such person can be found, there is no validating life; an interest for which there is no validating life is invalid.

In searching for a validating life, there is no formal rule forbidding the testing of anyone in the world to see if that person has the causal connection demanded by the requirement of initial certainty. There is, for example, no law against testing your favorite movie star or rock star in each case, if you want to do that. But experience has shown that no outsider will pass the test.

What we mean to say is that you can safely limit the persons you test to insiders—those who are connected in some way to the transaction. Only insiders have a chance of supplying the requisite causal connection demanded by the requirement of initial certainty. The insiders to be tested vary from situation to situation, but would always include: the transferor; the beneficiaries of the disposition, including but not restricted to the taker or takers of the challenged interest; the objects and donee of a power of appointment; persons related to the foregoing by blood or adoption, especially in the ascending and descending lines; and anyone else who has any connection to the transaction. If there is any doubt about a particular person, no harm is done by subjecting that person to the test. Usually it takes no more than an instant to resolve whether or not a person arguably on the fringe of the transaction has the requisite causal connection demanded by the requirement of initial certainty.

There is, however, no point in even considering the life of a complete outsider who is clearly unconnected to the transaction—a person selected at random from the world at large—just because the outsider happened to be in being at the creation of the interest. Outsiders in that category have already been tested and found *always* to be wanting. No outsider can possibly fulfill the requirement of initial certainty because there will always be an invalidating chain of possible post-creation events as to every outsider who might be proposed: any outsider can immediately die after the creation of the interest without having any effect on when the interest will vest or terminate.

Example 5.1: G devised land "to my son *A* for life, remainder to *A*'s children who live to age 21."

The interest in question is the contingent remainder in *A*'s children. To determine whether that interest is valid, you must test the insiders in this transaction to see if any of them satisfies the requirement of initial certainty. If yes, that person is the validating life. The obvious candidate to test is *A*. *A* satisfies the requirement of initial certainty here, because none of *A*'s children can reach 21 (or die under 21) beyond 21 years after *A*'s death.

Example 5.2: G devised land "to my daughter
B for life, remainder to *A*'s children who live to
age 21."

The obvious insiders to test first in this case
are *A* and *B*. Although *B* is the life tenant, she
does not satisfy the requirement of initial
certainty. A chain of possible post-creation
events that disqualifies her is that *A* might have
a child who reaches 21 (or dies under 21) more
than 21 years after her death. *A* does satisfy the
requirement of initial certainty, as we saw in
the previous example. This remains true here,
even though he is not a devisee.

In appropriate cases, the validating life need not
be individuated. Rather, the life can be a member
of a group of individuals. It is common in these
cases to say that the members of the group are the
validating *lives*. This is acceptable, as long as it is
recognized that the true meaning of the statement
is that the validating *life* is the life of the member
of the group who turns out to live the longest. As
was said in *Skatterwood v. Edge*, 1 Salk. 229, 91
Eng. Rep. 203 (K.B. 1697), "for let the lives be
never so many, there must be a survivor, and so it
is but the length of that life; for [Justice] Twisden
used to say, the candles were all lighted at once."

Example 5.3: G devised land "to my grandchildren who live to age 21."

The grandchildren's springing executory interest does not violate the common-law Rule. The validating life is the longest to live of *G*'s children. It is impossible for any of *G*'s grandchildren to reach 21 or die under 21 more than 21 years after the death of *G*'s last surviving child.

A well established but sometimes overlooked point is that the recipient of an interest might be the validating life. This point is especially useful where an interest is contingent on the recipient's reaching an age in excess of 21 or is contingent on the recipient's survival of a particular point in time that is or may be in excess of 21 years after the interest was created or after the death of a person in being at the date of creation.

Example 5.4: G devised land "to *A*'s children who are living 25 years after my death." *A* predeceased *G*. At *G*'s death, *A* had three living children.

The executory interest created in *A*'s children does not violate the common-law Rule. *A*'s children are their own validating lives. Each child will either survive the 25-year period or fail to do so within his or her own lifetime. To say this another way, we will know no later than at the death of each child whether or not that child survived the required period.

Dispositions of property sometimes create more than one interest that is subject to the Rule. When this happens, you must test the validity of each interest separately. A life that validates one interest might or might not validate the other interests. Consequently, you must search for a validating life for each interest.

§ 5.7 Time of Creation

The time when a property interest is created is important because it fixes the time when the validating life must be "in being." It is also important because it demarks the facts that can be taken into account in determining the validity of an interest. Under the common-law Rule, an interest is valid only if at the time when the interest is created, with the facts *then existing* taken into account, the interest is certain to vest or terminate within a life in being plus 21 years. The facts that actually occur from that time forward are irrelevant; all that counts is what *might* happen.

Property interests created by will are created when the testator dies, not when the testator signs the will. Thus the validating life for testamentary transfers must be a person who was alive (or in gestation) when the testator died, and the facts that can be taken into account in determining the validity of an interest created by will are those existing at the testator's death.

Property interests created by inter vivos transfers are created when the transfers become effective for purposes of property law generally. In most cases, this occurs when the deed conveying the property is delivered to the transferee(s), for this is the point at which the transfer becomes irrevocable. Consistent with this principle, property interests in revocable inter vivos trusts are considered created for perpetuity purposes when the power to revoke expires, typically at the death of the settlor of the trust.

§ 5.8   Class Gifts

A class gift is a gift to persons who are described by a group label, such as "children" or "descendants," and who are intended to take as a group. A typical feature of a class gift is that the membership of the group is able to increase or decrease, meaning that persons can be added or dropped as events (such as births, adoptions, or deaths) unfold in the future.

A gift is likely a class gift if the group members are *only* identified by a group label (such as "my children"). See Restatement 3d of Property § 13.1 cmt. g.

A gift is likely *not* a class gift, despite a group label, if the takers are also identified by name (such as "my children, *A*, *B*, and *C*"). Instead, this disposition is typically considered as a series of separate gifts of a fractional share of the property. See Restatement 3d of Property § 13.2 cmt. c.

The law treats these as presumptions that can be rebutted if "the language or circumstances indicate that the transferor intended" a contrary result. Restatement 3d of Property § 13.1(b), 13.2 (c). But the case law shows that the presumptions are seldom rebutted in practice. Accordingly, the examples in this *Nutshell* assume that the presumptions have not been rebutted.

A typical feature of a class gift is the ability of the group to fluctuate in number. This can occur through an *increase* in the number of takers (caused by births or adoptions) and/or through a *decrease* in the number of takers (caused by deaths).

The ability to fluctuate in number does not continue forever. Births, adoptions, or deaths can cause fluctuations only if they occur within a finite period of time. As a general proposition, once the time of possession has arrived, fluctuation comes to an end. However, as we shall see, this is only a general proposition, and the time limit on increase and the time limit on decrease are not always identical. That is, the ability of a given class gift to increase might expire before its ability to decrease, and vice versa. The point is that each time limit must be analyzed separately. Identifying these time limits is a crucial preliminary step toward determining the validity of the class gift under the Rule Against Perpetuities, for as we shall see, a class gift violates the common-law Rule if the gift is subject to increase or decrease beyond a life in being plus 21 years.

A class gift is *subject to decrease* if the gift is subject to a requirement of survival. A class member who fails to fulfill a requirement of survival drops out of the class. But there is an additional consequence: his or her lost share is added to the shares of the other members of the class who do become entitled to participate. This feature is intrinsic to class gifts—the built-in or implicit *gift over* to the other members of the class.

In the case of *testamentary* transfers, only devisees who survive the testator are entitled to take. This implicit requirement of survival is imposed by the common law, and applies to class gifts and individual gifts alike. The difference between class gifts and individual gifts arises from the fact that there is no built-in gift over to the other takers in the case of individual gifts. Consider the following example.

> *Example 5.5:* G devised land "to my children in equal shares." When the will was executed, G had three children (*A*, *B*, and *C*). *A* predeceased G. *B* and *C* survived G.
>
> Because G's will created a class gift, *B* and *C* each take an undivided one-half interest in the devised land.
>
> If G's will had created individual gifts ("to my three children, *A*, *B*, and *C*"), *A*'s lost one-third share would not have been added to the shares of *B* and *C*; it would have passed to G's residuary devisees or, in the absence of an effective residuary clause, to G's heirs.

Because a class gift such as the one in the preceding example is an immediate testamentary gift in fee simple absolute, it is subject to decrease between the time of the execution of the will and the time of the testator's death. Once the testator has died, the ability to decrease comes to an end. Thus, if after *G*'s death *B* dies survived by *C*, *B*'s one-half interest would not be divested in favor of *C*.

Suppose, however, that the class gift is a *future* interest rather than an immediate one in fee simple absolute. Here the question of whether the ability to decrease continues beyond the testator's death depends on whether a condition of survival is attached to the class gift.

Example 5.6: *G* devised land "to *A* for life, remainder to *A*'s children." *G* was survived by *A* and by *A*'s three children (*X*, *Y*, and *Z*). *Z* died during *A*'s lifetime. *X* and *Y* survived *A*.

The class (consisting of *X*, *Y*, and *Z* as of *G*'s death) is not allowed to decrease beyond *G*'s death. The reason is that no express condition of survival was attached to the children's remainder interest.[2] Consequently, upon A's death, X, Y, and Z (i.e., Z's successor in interest) each take an undivided one-third share in the devised land. Z does not drop out of the class because of her death between the deaths of G and A.

If G's will had expressly imposed a condition of survival ("to A for life, remainder to A's children who survive A"), then the class would have continued to be subject to decrease beyond G's death. On these facts, Z would have dropped out of the class. Z's lost one-third share would have been added to the shares of X and Y. Upon A's death, X and Y would each receive an undivided one-half share in the

---

[2]This analysis is based on the common-law rule that a future interest is not subject to a condition of survival of the life tenant unless one is expressly imposed. This rule may be changed by statute. UPC § 2-707, for example, presumptively makes all future interests *in trust* subject to a condition precedent of survival and provides that the deceased person's surviving descendants take the share that the deceased person would have taken had he or she survived; thus under this statute, had G's devise been in trust, Z's one-third share would be divided among Z's descendants who survived A, and would go to X and Y only if Z left no such descendants.

devised land.[3]

Thus far, we have been discussing a decrease in the number of takers of a class gift. The number of takers is also able to *increase*. The following example develops the difference between class gifts and individual gifts on this point.

Example 5.7: G devised land "to my children." When the will was executed, G had two children, A and B. Later G had a third child, C. G was survived by all three children.

Because G's will created a class gift, A, B, and C each take an undivided one-third share in the devised land.

If G's will had created individual gifts ("to my children, A and B"), the result would have been different. The shares of A and B would have remained constant at one-half each.[4]

---

[3]This analysis is based on the common law. Had G's devise been in trust, UPC § 2-707 provides that Z's one-third share would be divided among Z's descendants who survived A, and would go to X and Y only if Z left no such descendants.

[4]This analysis is based on the common law. UPC § 2-302 provides that C would take an equal share in the devised land unless it is proved that G intentionally excluded C. Statutes in nearly all non-UPC states provide that C would take an

A class is subject to increase—subject to open—as long as new entrants can come into the class. The ability of a class to increase ends—the class "closes"—at the *earlier* of two events: (1) the natural (or physiological) closing of the class;[5] or (2) the artificial (or premature) closing brought about by the application of the rule of convenience.

The natural closing of a class occurs when births (or, if adopted members are within the class description, adoptions) become physiologically impossible. A class gift in favor of a transferor's grandchildren physiologically closes upon the death of the transferor's last living child. A grandchild who is in gestation on the date the class closes is regarded as in being on the closing date.

---

intestate share unless it is proved that *G* intentionally excluded *C*; *C*'s intestate share would ordinarily be paid out of *G*'s residuary estate rather than out of the devised land.

[5]Under traditional property law, death is deemed to terminate the possibility of having children. New technologies, however, make it possible in practice to have children by assisted reproduction after death. The Restatement 3d of Property § 15.1 cmt. j adopts a new rule that such children "be treated as in being at the decedent's death, for purposes of the class-closing rules, if the child was born within a reasonable time after the decedent's death."

A class may close earlier than its physiological closing. When this happens, the class has been closed artificially. Artificial closing is governed by the *rule of convenience.*

The rule of convenience is a rule of construction, not a rule of law. It yields to a contrary intent. In practice, however, a contrary intent can seldom be shown, and consequently the rule of convenience typically prevails.

Once a class has been closed by the rule of convenience, subsequently conceived or adopted persons are not entitled to participate in the class gift, even though they otherwise fit the class label. New entrants come into a class only if they are conceived[6] or adopted[7] while the class is still open.

The rule of convenience holds that a class closes when a class member becomes entitled to distribution of a share. This rule is founded on two basic premises. First is the premise that the use of only a group or class description indicates that all

---

[6] A child in gestation when a class closes is regarded as in being at that time. To enter the class, the child must be born alive and probably must be born viable.

[7] With respect to an adopted child, the date of adoption, not the date of conception, is the significant date.

persons who fit the description, whenever born or adopted, were intended to share in the gift. In other words, the starting point is that the class was not intended to close until it closes naturally. Second, because of inherent difficulties or "inconveniences" in allowing participation by persons born or adopted after distribution, it is believed that the transferor, if the transferor had contemplated the difficulties, would have intended to exclude these persons. That is, although the basic intent of the transferor is to keep the class open until it closes naturally, if inconveniences will arise from doing so, the transferor would prefer for the class to be closed prematurely, so that the inconveniences will be avoided.

The inconvenience of a class being kept open after distribution is that the distributees would not take an indefeasible interest. Instead, they would receive a considerably less useful defeasible one. Taking an interest that is subject to being partially divested upon the birth or adoption of additional class members would render the property less marketable and, if personal property, would require some device such as the posting of security to protect the interests of unborn or unadopted members of the class.

Example 5.8: G devised land "to my grandchildren." When G executed her will, her only child, A, had a child, X. Later, but before G's death, A had a second child, Y. G then died, survived by A, X, and Y.

Under the rule of convenience, the class remains open until G's death but closes when G died even though A is alive and therefore is deemed capable of having more children. X and Y each take an undivided estate in one half of the devised land in fee simple absolute. In other words, their estates are not subject to partial divestment in favor of any later-born or later-adopted children of A.

The rule of convenience does not operate if there is no class member entitled to distribution.

Example 5.9: G devised land "to my grandchildren." At G's death, G's only child A was alive but had no children.

The rule of convenience does not close the class at G's death. Rather, the class remains open until it closes naturally, at A's death. The only feasible alternative would be to nullify the class gift entirely. It is thought that few testators would desire this result.

The same principles apply to class gifts in which possession is postponed—i.e., to future interests created in a class. Consider the following example.

Example 5.10: G devised land "to A for life, remainder to B's children." G was survived by A, B, and B's child, X. B later had a second child, Y, during A's lifetime, and a third child, Z, after A's death.

The class continues to be subject to increase beyond G's death and during A's lifetime. It closes on A's death even though B is still alive and is deemed capable of having more children. X and Y will clearly be able to participate. Z will be entitled to participate only if Z was in gestation at A's death.

Suppose instead that by the time of A's death no children had been born to B and that none was then in gestation. This situation is treated consistently with Example 5.9. The class would not close at A's death but rather would remain open until it closes physiologically—at B's death.

We can now turn to the application of the Rule Against Perpetuities to class gifts. The governing principle is the all-or-nothing rule, which we encountered earlier in § 5.3. That rule states: *If the interest of any potential class member might vest too remotely, the entire class gift is invalid.* In other words, a class gift is either completely valid or completely invalid. It is not permissible to treat the interest of each class member separately and say that some class members have valid interests and other class members have invalid interests. See Restatement of Property §§ 371, 383, 384.

Example 5.11: G devised land "to *A* for life, then to *A*'s children who live to age 25." *G* was survived by *A* and by *A*'s two children, *X* and *Y*. *X* had reached 25 at *G*'s death, but *Y* was under 25.

The class gift in *A*'s children who reach 25 is invalid. *X* and *Y* are their own validating lives, but there is no validating life for children born to or adopted by *A* after *G*'s death. Note that the rule of convenience does not close the class at *G*'s death, because the time of distribution for *A*'s children is *A*'s death, not *G*'s death.

Two types of class gifts are exempt from the all-or-nothing rule: specific-sum class gifts and gifts to sub-classes. These special types of class gifts are exempt because the rationale of the all-or-nothing rule does not apply to them. Accordingly, each interest can be judged separately; the invalidity of one interest does not affect the validity of another.

Specific-sum class gifts give a specific amount of money to each class member, for example "$10,000 to each of my grandchildren who reach 25." This is different from the conventional class gift, wherein a sum of money or item of property is to be divided proportionally among the class members.

Gifts to sub-classes involve the subdivision of a class gift into separate shares, for example "to each of *A*'s children for their respective lives, and on the death of each child the proportionate share of corpus of the one so dying shall go to the children of such child."

In each case, the rationale of the all-or-nothing rule does not apply, because the transferor has divided the gift such that the interest of one class member (or sub-class) does not impinge on another.

§ 5.9   Constructional Preference for Validity

Professor Gray stated that a will or deed is to be construed without regard to the Rule Against

Perpetuities, and then the Rule is to be applied "remorselessly" to the provisions so construed. Gray on Perpetuities § 629. Some courts may still adhere to this proposition. Most courts, we believe, would now be inclined to adopt the proposition put forward by the Restatement of Property § 375, which is that where an instrument is ambiguous—that is, where it is fairly susceptible to two or more constructions, one of which causes a Rule violation and the other of which does not—the construction that does not result in a Rule violation should be adopted.

One manifestation of the constructional preference for validity is the *principle of separability*, which courts invoke when an interest is subject to alternative contingencies, one of which causes a Rule violation. Suppose, for example, that property is devised "to *B* if X-event or Y-event happens." If there is no validating life for X-event but there is one for Y-event, courts will typically strike the invalid contingency so that the devise is altered to read "to *B* if Y-event happens." Consider the following example.

Example 5.12: G devised the residue of his estate "to *A* for life, then to *A*'s children who survive A and live to age 25, but if none of A's children survives A or if none of A's children who survives A lives to age 25, then to B." G was survived by A.

The class gift in A's children is invalid and is replaced by a reversion in G's heirs.

What about B's executory interest? The separability principle divides it into two interests: one contingent on none of A's children surviving A, and the other contingent on none of A's children who survives A living to age 25. The first of these, but not the second, is valid. Consequently, the language "or if none of A's children who survives A lives to age 25" is in effect stricken from the devise. B takes if none of A's children survives A.

Because the separability principle saves one of B's executory interests, the reversion in G's heirs is vested subject to divestment in favor of B if none of A's children survives A.

Note that the principle of separability is applicable only when the transferor has *expressly* stated the contingencies in the alternative. Where alternative contingencies are merely implicit, no separation will be recognized. In the words of Sir George Jessel, Master of the Rolls, in *Miles v. Harford*, 12

Ch.D. 691 (Ch. 1879), "that is what [the courts] mean by splitting, they will not split the expression by dividing the two events, but when they find two expressions they give effect to both of them as if you had struck the other out of the will." Consider the following example.

Example 5.13: G devised the residue of his estate "to *A* for life, then to *A*'s children who survive *A* and live to age 25, but if none of *A*'s children does so, then to *B*." *A* survived *G*.

The class gift in *A*'s children is invalid and is replaced by a reversion in *G*'s heirs.

What about *B*'s executory interest? The separability principle cannot apply, because *B*'s interest is subject to one condition precedent, not two, namely the condition that "none of *A*'s children does so." Accordingly *B*'s interest is completely invalid, and the reversion in *G*'s heirs is indefeasibly vested.

§ 5.10   Consequences of Invalidity

When an interest is invalid because it violates the common-law Rule Against Perpetuities, the invalid interest is stricken from the disposition. Unless the doctrine of infectious invalidity (see below) applies, the other interests created by the disposition (assuming that none of them violates the Rule) take effect as if the invalid interest had never been created.

Example 5.14: G devised real property "to *A* for life, then to *A*'s children for the life of the survivor, and upon the death of *A*'s last surviving child, to *A*'s grandchildren." *G* devised her residuary estate to her husband, *H*. *G* was survived by *A* and *H*.

Due to the invalidity of the remainder to *A*'s grandchildren, the disposition reads as if that remainder interest had never been created: "to *A* for life, then to *A*'s children for the life of the survivor." Since *G*'s devise did not validly dispose of all interests in the parcel of real property, the undisposed-of interest passes under *G*'s residuary clause to *H*. This testamentary transfer of the remainder interest to *H* is deemed to have occurred at *G*'s death. Thus when *A*'s last surviving child dies, the property goes to *H* (or *H*'s successor in interest).

Note that if *G*'s original devise had been in her residuary clause, the undisposed-of interest would have been intestate property and would have passed at *G*'s death to her heirs.

Example 5.15: G devised land "to *A* for life, then for life to such of *A*'s children as reach 25, then to *B*." *G* was survived by *A* and *B*.

The remainder for life to *A*'s children is invalid. The effect of striking it is not to create a gap that must be filled by the residuary clause. Rather it is to accelerate *B*'s remainder; the devise now reads "to *A* for life, then to *B*."

In appropriate cases, the invalidity of an interest may, under the *doctrine of infectious invalidity*, be held to invalidate one or more otherwise valid interests created by the disposition, or even invalidate the entire disposition. The question turns on whether the general dispositive scheme of the transferor will be better carried out by elimination of only the invalid interest or by elimination of other interests as well.

This is a question that must be answered on a case by case basis. Several items are relevant to the question, including who takes the stricken interests in place of the persons designated by the transferor. Some jurisdictions have become noted for a greater willingness to apply infectious invalidity than others. The following example is loosely based on *Taylor v. Dooley*, 297 S.W.2d 905 (Ky. 1956).

Example 5.16: G was survived by his two children, *A* and *B*. *G*'s will divided his property in half, devising one half to *A* outright and the other half "to *B* for life, then to *B*'s children who live to the age of 30."

The remainder in *B*'s children is invalid. The usual response would be to strike the remainder, thus creating an undisposed-of interest that would pass at *G*'s death to his heirs, presumably *A* and *B*. This would have the effect of increasing *A*'s eventual share to three fourths and reducing the share passing to *B*'s successors (presumably her children) to one fourth. Rather than permit this sizeable inequality, a court might conclude that it would be more consistent with *G*'s intention to apply the doctrine of infectious invalidity, striking all gifts created by the will, thus causing *G*'s property to pass by intestacy to *A* and *B* equally.

§ 5.11 Policy of the Rule

What is the purpose of the Rule Against Perpetuities? Professor Lewis Simes tackled this question in his article on The Policy Against Perpetuities, 103 U. Pa. L. Rev. 707 (1955). Simes identified four public policies that have been used to justify the Rule: (1) furthering the alienability of property, (2) enhancing the productivity of property, (3) preventing undue concentrations of wealth, and (4) prohibiting excessive dead-hand control. Simes argued, correctly, that the first two of these policies have little force in the modern era, because future interests are now mainly created in trusts, not directly in land (recall § 1.4). The trustee has the power to sell and reinvest trust assets, and the duty to make trust assets productive. The third of these policies also has less force, because we use (or can use) federal transfer taxation to limit wealth concentration. The fourth policy is the one that remains in force. In the words of Professor Simes, "the Rule Against Perpetuities strikes a fair balance between the desires of members of the present generation, and similar desires of succeeding generations, to do what they wish with the property which they enjoy." (For a critique, see T.P. Gallanis, The Rule Against Perpetuities and the Law Commission's Flawed Philosophy, 59 Camb. L. J. 284 (2000).)

Where is this "fair balance" to be drawn? Sir Arthur Hobhouse suggested a know-and-see theory: "A clear, obvious, natural line is drawn for us between those persons and events which the Settlor knows and sees, and those which he cannot know or see." Arthur Hobhouse, The Dead Hand 188 (1880). Professors Leach and Tudor expanded on the know-and-see test: "In a will a man of property could provide for all of those in his family whom he personally knew and the first generation after them upon attaining majority." W. Barton Leach & Owen Davies Tudor, The Common Law Rule Against Perpetuities, in Am. L. Prop. § 24.16. A further refinement of the theory has been suggested: "[T]he [know-and-see] standard [arguably means] that donors should be allowed to exert control through the youngest generation of descendants they knew and saw, or at least one or more but not necessarily all of whom they knew and saw." Lawrence W. Waggoner, The Uniform Statutory Rule Against Perpetuities, 21 Real. Prop., Prob. & Trust J. 569 (1986).

As you study the material in this chapter, and especially as you work through the examples, keep in mind the know-and-see theory. Does the Rule effectively balance the interests of present and succeeding generations?

§ 5.12   Technical Violations

The required certainty that an interest will vest or terminate within a life in being plus 21 years has invalidated some interests even though they do not appear to violate the policy of the Rule. That is, the policy of the Rule would not seem to apply to such cases because, realistically speaking, the likelihood that the interest will remain contingent beyond the perpetuity period is remote. These cases have been labeled "technical violations." These cases fall generally into three categories, discussed in a famous article by Professor W. Barton Leach, Perpetuities in a Nutshell, 51 Harv. L. Rev. 638 (1938): (1) the fertile octogenarian, (2) the after-born spouse (termed by Leach the "unborn widow"), and (3) the administrative contingency.

The case of the fertile octogenarian refers to the Rule's presumption of lifetime fertility and how it interacts with the all-or-nothing rule of class gifts. Regardless of real-world facts, the Rule presumes that people are capable of having children until the moment of death. Yet the possibility of after-born children entering a class can be sufficient to render the class gift invalid. Consider the following example.

Example 5.17: G devised the residue of his estate in trust, directing the trustee to pay the income "to *A* for life, then to *A*'s children for the life of the survivor, and upon the death of *A*'s last surviving child, to pay the corpus of the trust to *A*'s then-living grandchildren." *G* was survived by *A* and *A*'s two children, *X* and *Y*.

The remainder in *A*'s grandchildren is invalid because of the possibility that *A* might have a third child, *Z*, who might have a child (a grandchild of *A*) conceived and born more than 21 years after the death of the lives in being: *A*, *X*, and *Y*.

What if, in this example, the possibility of *A* having a third child, *Z*, was zero, because *A* was infertile having passed the menopause, or because *A* had undergone a hysterectomy (or, if male, a vasectomy)? The answer is that such facts are irrelevant to the common-law Rule Against Perpetuities. For purposes of the common-law Rule, early English decisions, of which *Jee v. Audley*, 1 Cox's Ch. Cas. 324, 29 Eng. Rep. 1186 (Ch. 1787), is the best known, laid down the proposition that all persons are conclusively presumed to be capable of having children throughout their lifetimes, regardless of age or physical condition. In that case, Sir Lloyd Kenyon, the Master of the Rolls, stated:

> I am desired to do in this case something which I do not feel myself at liberty to do, namely to suppose it impossible for persons in so advanced an age as John and Elizabeth Jee [both age 70] to have children; but if this can be done in one case it may in another, and it is a very dangerous experiment, and introductive of the greatest inconvenience to give a latitude to such sort of conjecture.

This presumption of lifetime fertility makes more sense than might originally appear. In the modern era, one must also consider the possibility of having children by adoption. The trend in modern law is strongly in favor of including adopted children in class gifts (see, for example, Uniform Probate Code § 2-705), and even elderly or infirm people can adopt.

In some instances, a way around the fertile octogenarian problem might be found in perpetuity law's general constructional preference for validity. If the possibility of future children was remote when the transferor executed the document, a court might hold that the transferor never intended to include after-born or after-adopted children within the class gift. With such children excluded, the Rule's requirement of initial certainty would be met, and the class gift valid. It is worth noting, however, that this strategy depends on what the transferor knew at the time the document was executed. In Example 5.17, if *A* were a 25-year old female in good physical condition when *G* signed the will, it would be hard to claim that *G* intended to exclude after-born or after-adopted children. It is also worth noting that some courts have been unwilling to use the general constructional preference for validity to overcome fertile octogenarian problems.

If adults are conclusively presumed to be able to have children, are children below the age of puberty (referred to by Professor Leach as "precocious toddlers") also subject to this presumption? Cases raising this question are rare, but they do seem to extend the presumption of fertility to one's entire lifetime. See *Rust v. Rust*, 147 Tex. 181, 211 S.W.2d 262, aff'd, 214 S.W.2d 246 (1948) (court assumed for perpetuity purposes that a 9-year old daughter would be able to have a child before her 14th birthday).

The second technical violation arises in the case of the after-born spouse. This term refers to the fact that an unnamed "spouse," "surviving spouse," "widow," or "widower" is excluded from serving as the validating life, because such person *might* have been conceived and born after the creation of the interest. Consider the following example.

> *Example 5.18:* G devised land "to my son *A* for life, remainder to his widow for life, remainder to *A*'s then-living descendants." *G* was survived by *A*, *A*'s wife *W*, and their adult children *X* and *Y*.
>
> The remainder in *A*'s descendants is invalid. Though improbable, it is possible that *A*'s widow will not be *W* but someone born after *G*'s death, who thus cannot serve as a validating life.

In some cases, the general constructional preference for validity has been used to avoid the after-born spouse problem. When the dispositive language fairly allows, some courts have construed the reference to *A*'s "widow," "widower," "spouse," or "surviving spouse," as a reference to the person to whom *A* was married when the will was executed or when *G* died (in this example, *W*).

Of course, this is easier to do with terms such as "spouse," "husband," or "wife," than with terms that import an element of survivorship such as "widow," "widower," or "surviving spouse."

The third technical violation arises in the case of the administrative contingency, which refers to the performance by a fiduciary (an executor or trustee) of some administrative function which *might* take more than 21 years. Typical examples are the completion of the probate of a will, the settlement of an estate, the payment of debts or taxes, the sale of estate assets, or the delivery of trust corpus on the termination of a trust. Consider the following example.

Example 5.19: G devised land "to my grandchildren, born before or after my death, who are living upon final distribution of my estate."

By the majority view, the grandchildren's interest is invalid. Though unlikely, there is a possibility that final distribution will not occur within 21 years after G's death. This possibility means that no life can validate the interest. Grandchildren may be conceived and born after G's death, and such after-born grandchildren may survive the final distribution of *G*'s estate (or fail to do so) beyond 21 years after the deaths of the children and grandchildren in being at the creation of the interest.

As this example illustrates, the term "administrative contingency" is somewhat misleading. The term does not refer to the possibility that the administrative task will never be completed. Rather, it is accepted that the task will be completed, presumably because of the fiduciary's legal obligation to do so. The uncertainty is the length of time it might take to finish the job.

A minority of courts has devised an escape from the administrative contingency problem. These courts hold that the fiduciary's obligation is to complete the task within a reasonable time, meaning less than 21 years. The difficulty with this minority view is that it is a fiction to say that the settlement of an estate can *never* take more than 21 years without violating a fiduciary duty. While rare, there can be cases in which protracted and successive litigation over a multitude of issues legitimately ties up an estate for a very long time.

§ 5.13 Perpetuity Saving Clauses

The common-law Rule is less fearsome to practicing estate-planning lawyers than it is to law students and law graduates studying for the bar examination. This is not because lawyers have found that the Rule becomes more understandable with experience, although that is also true, but because they have discovered that they need not be greatly concerned about the Rule's effect on their clients' plans because they use perpetuity saving clauses.

A typical perpetuity saving clause might provide:

The trust hereby created shall terminate in any event not later than 21 years after the death of the last survivor of my descendants who are in being at the time this instrument becomes effective, *and unless sooner terminated by the terms hereof, the trustee shall, at the termination of such period, make distribution to the persons then entitled to the income of this trust, and in the same shares and proportions as they are so entitled.*

Formulated and used properly, perpetuity saving clauses mean that no lawyer need ever fear that a trust or other property arrangement will violate the common-law Rule. These clauses do not typically govern the term of the trust; they operate as a back-stop just in case the actual term of the trust exceeds the time allotted by the saving clause. The part of the clause that establishes this period of time is called the *perpetuity-period component*. Saving clauses also contain a second component, called the *gift-over component*, that expressly creates a gift guaranteed to vest at the termination of the period established in the perpetuity-period component but only if the interests have neither vested nor terminated earlier in accordance with their primary terms. In the sample saving clause above, the perpetuity-period component is underlined, and the gift-over component is in italics.

It needs to be stressed that a saving clause measures off a true "perpetuity period." The persons designated in a saving clause must be kept track of in order to determine when the last surviving member of the group dies.

In most cases, the saving clause not only avoids a violation of the common-law Rule; it also, in a sense, over-insures the client's disposition against the possibility that the gift over will ever take effect. The period of time established by the perpetuity-period component usually provides a margin of safety, because most trusts terminate on their own before the end of the perpetuity period would be reached. The clause, therefore, is usually a formality that validates the disposition without affecting the substance of the disposition.

§ 5.14   Perpetuity Reform

The need for perpetuity reform is not much in doubt, but controversy persists about the method. Three basic methods have been advanced: (1) discrete statutory repair of the technical violations discussed above in § 5.12, along with reduction of age contingencies to 21; (2) immediately available reformation; and (3) wait-and-see, with deferred reformation (reformation only if an interest remains contingent at the expiration of the permissible vesting period).

New York and Illinois have enacted legislative provisions that effect a *discrete statutory repair* of the technical violations discussed in § 5.12; they also reduce age contingencies to 21, thereby removing the need for beneficiaries of future interests to be their own validating lives. Let us take the New York statutes by way of example.

Under New York law: (1) males below 14 and females below 13 or above 55 are presumed incapable of having children, evidence is admissible regarding the actual inability to bear children, and the possibility of having a child by adoption is disregarded; (2) an interest in the spouse of another person is presumed to refer to a person living at the date the Rule commences to run; (3) administrative contingencies are presumed to be completed within the perpetuity period; and (4) where an interest would be invalid because it depends upon a person attaining or failing to attain an age exceeding 21 years, the age shall be reduced to 21. N.Y. Est., Powers & Tr. Law §§ 9-1.2, 9-1.3. Illinois has similar but not identical provisions. 765 Ill. Comp. Stat. § 305/3.

A few states have enacted statutes authorizing or directing *immediate reformation* of dispositions that violate the common-law Rule. Oklahoma's statute is representative:

Any interest in real or personal property that would violate the rule against perpetuities shall be reformed, or construed within the limits of the rule, to give effect to the general intent of the creator of that interest whenever that general intent can be ascertained. This provision shall be liberally construed and applied to validate such interest to the fullest extent consistent with such ascertained intent.

The difficulty with immediate reformation is that it requires up-front litigation as a regular matter.

A far preferable approach is *wait-and-see with deferred reformation*. Indeed, we believe we are accurate in reporting that this is the only realistic hope for widespread perpetuity reform (short of abolition, on which see § 5.16).

Under the common-law Rule, the validity of a future interest depends on the full array of possible post-creation events. Why not instead take actual post-creation events into account? Instead of invalidating an interest because of what *might* happen, waiting to see what *does* happen seems much more sensible. Known as the wait-and-see method of perpetuity reform, this approach is the approach promulgated by the two preeminent national organizations concerned with law reform—the American Law Institute, in its Restatement 2d of Property (1983), and the National Conference of Commissioners on Uniform State Laws, in the Uniform Statutory Rule

Against Perpetuities (1986, amended modestly in 1990).

Neither the ALI's Restatement 2d of Property nor NCCUSL's Uniform Rule alters what may be called the *validating* side of the common-law Rule. Dispositions that would have been valid under the common-law Rule remain valid. Practitioners under either wait-and-see regime can and should continue to use a traditional perpetuity saving clause. The wait-and-see element is applied only to interests that fall prey to the *invalidating* side of the common-law Rule. Interests that would be invalid at common law are saved from being rendered *initially invalid*. To prevent the unjust enrichment of unintended takers caused by a drafter's mistake in failing to insert an appropriate perpetuity saving clause, otherwise invalid interests are, as it were, given a second chance: these interests are valid if they actually vest within the permissible vesting period and become invalid only if they remain in existence but still contingent at the expiration of that period.

Wait-and-see should be thought of as a perpetuity saving clause injected by law. The permissible vesting period under wait-and-see is, or should be, the equivalent of the perpetuity-period component of a well-conceived saving clause. Recall, too, that the saving clause includes a gift-over component. Deferred reformation is the near-equivalent, providing for judicial reformation of a disposition in case the interest is still in existence but contingent when the permissible vesting period expires.

Shifting the focus from possible to actual post-creation events has great attraction, and wait-and-see has been widely adopted, though still opposed by a few academics. The greatest controversy over wait-and-see concerns how the permissible vesting period is to be marked off—the permissible period of time for the contingencies attached to an otherwise invalid interest to be finally resolved.

The Restatement 2d of Property § 1.3(2) uses a predetermined list of measuring lives. The permissible vesting period expires 21 years after the death of the survivor of:

(a) The transferor if the period of the rule begins to run in the transferor's lifetime; and

(b) Those individuals alive when the period of the rule begins to run, if reasonable in number, who have beneficial interests vested or contingent in the property in which the non-vested interest in question exists and the parents and grandparents alive when the period of the rule begins to run of all beneficiaries of the property in which the non-vested interest exists; and

(c) The donee of a nonfiduciary power of appointment alive when the period of the rule begins to run if the exercise of such power could affect the non-vested interest in question.

If a property interest is still in existence but contingent at the expiration of the permissible vesting period, Restatement 2d of Property § 1.5 provides that "the transferred property shall be disposed of in the manner which most closely effectuates the transferor's manifested plan of distribution and which is within the limits of the rule against perpetuities."

So far, the Restatement's version of wait-and-see has not been directly adopted by any court or legislature, although it did influence a provision of Iowa law. See Iowa Code § 558.68.

The general contour of the Uniform Rule is similar to that of the Restatement 2d of Property. The validating side of the common-law Rule is retained but the invalidating side is replaced with wait-and-see and deferred-reformation elements. The major departure from the Restatement approach is that the Uniform Rule uses a flat 90-year vesting period, rather than a period ending 21 years after the death of the survivor of a predetermined list of measuring lives.

The Uniform Rule is currently in effect in Arizona, California, Colorado, Connecticut, the District of Columbia, Georgia, Hawaii, Indiana, Kansas, Massachusetts, Michigan, Minnesota, Montana, Nebraska, New Mexico, North Carolina, North Dakota, Oregon, South Carolina, Tennessee, Virginia,[8] and West Virginia.

At the heart of the Uniform Rule is § 1(a), which provides:

A nonvested property interest is invalid unless: (1) when the interest is created, it is certain to vest or terminate no later than 21 years after the death of an individual then alive; or (2) the

---

[8]Virginia adopted the Uniform Rule on April 8, 2000. See Va. Code § 55-12.1 et seq. On the same day, Virginia also made the Rule Against Perpetuities optional. See Va. Code § 55-13.3(e). For discussion, see § 5.16.

interest either vests or terminates within 90 years after its creation.

Interests that are invalid under the Uniform Rule are subject to reformation under § 3, which provides:

Upon the petition of an interested person, a court shall reform a disposition in the manner that most closely approximates the transferor's manifested plan of distribution and is within the 90 years allowed by [§ 1(a)] if: (1) a nonvested property interest or a power of appointment becomes invalid under [§ 1]; (2) a class gift is not but might become invalid under [§ 1] and the time has arrived when the share of any class member is to take effect in possession or enjoyment; or (3) a nonvested property interest that is not validated by [§ 1(a)] can vest but not within 90 years after its creation.

The most striking feature of the Uniform Rule is its use of a flat period of 90 years as the vesting period in its wait-and-see element. The rationale for this step was explained by the Reporter for the Uniform Rule, as follows:

[T]he philosophy behind the 90-year period was to fix a period of time that approximates the average period of time that would traditionally be allowed by the wait-and-see doctrine. There was no intention to use the flat-period-of-years method as a means of lengthening the [permissible vesting] period beyond its traditional boundaries. The fact that the traditional period roughly averages out to a longish-sounding 90 years is a reflection of a quite different phenomenon: the dramatic increase in longevity that society as a whole has experienced in the course of the twentieth century....

[T]he traditional method of delimiting the [permissible vesting] period [under earlier proposals for wait-and-see, including that of the Restatement 2d of Property] is to use actual measuring lives plus 21 years. Specifically, under this method, a group of persons—called the measuring lives—is identified. Once the group is identified, the lives of all its members are traced to see which one outlives all the others and when that survivor dies. The [permissible vesting] period extends 21 years beyond the death of that last surviving measuring life.

From its inception, the actual-measuring-lives approach has been plagued by two problems: identification and tracing. The identification problem concerns the method by which the measuring lives are to be chosen.... The second problem plaguing the actual-measuring-lives approach is that of tracing. No matter how the measuring lives are identified, the lives of those actual individuals must be traced to determine which one is the longest survivor and when he or she died....

By opting for a flat period of years, the framers of [the Uniform Rule] eliminated the clutter that has heretofore plagued the wait-and-see strategy—the problems of identifying, tracing, and possibly litigating the make-up of a sometimes-fluctuating group of measuring lives. The expiration of a [permissible vesting] period measured by a flat period of years is litigation free, easy to determine, and unmistakable....

In the normal course of events, the youngest measuring life is the key to the length of the [permissible vesting] period, and no matter which method is used for determining the identity of the measuring lives, the youngest measuring life, in standard trusts, is likely to be the transferor's youngest descendant living when the trust was created. The 90-year period of [the Uniform Rule] is premised on this proposition. Using four hypothetical families deemed to be representative of actual families, the framers determined that, on average, the transferor's youngest descendant in being at the transferor's death—assuming the transferor's death to occur between ages 60 and 90, which is when 73 percent of the population die—is about 6 years old. The remaining life expectancy of a 6-year old is about 69 years. The 69 years, plus the 21-year tack-on period, gives [a permissible vesting] period of 90 years. Although this method may not be scientifically accurate to the nth degree, the Drafting Committee considered it reliable enough to support a [permissible vesting] period of 90 years, given the margin-of-safety function that it performs.

Lawrence W. Waggoner, The Uniform Statutory Rule Against Perpetuities: The Rationale of the 90-Year Waiting Period, 73 Cornell L. Rev. 157, 162-68 (1988)(excerpted with the permission of the Cornell Law Review).

Section 3 of the Uniform Rule directs a court, upon the petition of an interested person, to reform a disposition within the limits of the 90-year permissible vesting period, in the manner deemed by the court most closely to approximate the transferor's manifested plan of distribution. The "interested person" who would frequently bring the reformation suit would be the trustee. Seldom will this section become operative. Of the fraction of trusts and other property arrangements that are incompetently drafted, and thus fail to meet the requirement of initial validity under the codified version of the validating side of the common-law Rule, almost all of them will have terminated by their own terms long before any of the circumstances requisite to reformation under § 3 arise.

If, against the odds, the right to reformation does arise, it will be found easier than perhaps anticipated to determine how best to reform the disposition. Note that reformation under § 3 is mandatory, not subject to the discretion of the court. Consequently, the common-law doctrine of infectious invalidity is superseded by the Uniform Rule. The court is given two reformation criteria: (1) the transferor's manifested plan of distribution, and (2) the 90-year permissible vesting period. Because governing instruments are where transferors manifest their plans of distribution, the imaginary horrible of courts being forced to probe the minds of long-dead transferors will not materialize.

The theory of § 3 is to defer the right to reformation until reformation becomes truly necessary. Thus, the basic rule of § 3(1) is that the right to reformation does not arise until a contingent property interest or a power of appointment becomes invalid; under § 1, this does not occur until the expiration of the 90-year permissible vesting period. By confining perpetuity litigation to those few cases in which the permissible vesting period actually is exceeded, perpetuity litigation is limited.

Example 5.20: G devised the residue of his estate in trust, directing the trustee to pay the income "to *A* for life, then to *A*'s children for the life of the survivor, and upon the death of *A*'s last surviving child, to pay the corpus of the trust to *A*'s then-living descendants, by representation."

The Uniform Rule allows 90 years for the

remainder to vest. If *A* still has one or more living children on the 90th anniversary of *G*'s death, the remainder interest becomes invalid. However, the disposition can be judicially reformed to make it valid.

The most appropriate form of reformation would be to vest the remainder interest in *A*'s descendants who would take if *A*'s last surviving child had died on the 90th anniversary of *G*'s death. This would not cut short the income interest of *A*'s living children. The remainder in *A*'s descendants would be vested in interest but not in possession. Possession would still be postponed until the actual death of *A*'s last surviving child.

In certain cases, the Uniform Rule grants the right to reformation *before* the 90-year period runs out. The Uniform Rule grants a right to early reformation when it becomes necessary to do so or when there is no point in waiting that period out. Thus, the Uniform Rule in § 3(2) grants a right to early reformation whenever the share of any class member is entitled to take effect in possession or enjoyment, even though the class gift is not yet but might still become invalid under wait-and-see.

Example 5.21: G devised property in trust, directing the trustee to pay the income "to *A* for life, then to *A*'s children"; the corpus of the trust is to be equally divided among *A*'s children who reach the age of 30. G was survived by *A* and by *A*'s two children *X* and *Y*, both of whom were under 30 when G died. After G's death, *A* had a third child, *Z*. *Z*'s age was such that he could be alive but under age 30 on the 90th anniversary of G's death. At *A*'s death, *X* and *Y* were over age 30.

The criteria for early reformation are met: (1) *X* and *Y* are entitled to possession of their shares as of *A*'s death; and (2) under the all-or-nothing rule applicable to class gifts, the class gift might become invalid because *Z* might reach 30 beyond the 90-year period after G's death.

The most appropriate form of reformation would be to make *Z*'s interest contingent on reaching, not age 30, but the 90th anniversary of G's death. This makes *Z*'s interest valid under the Uniform Rule and validates the entire class gift. Under this approach, *X* and *Y* are immediately entitled to receive their one-third shares. If *Z*'s interest later vests, *Z* would receive the remaining one-third share. If *Z* fails to reach the 90th anniversary of *G*'s death, the one-third share would instead be divided equally between *X* and *Y* or their successors.

The Uniform Rule also grants the right to early reformation in one other situation: if a contingent property interest can vest but not before the 90-year period has expired. Though unlikely, such a case can theoretically arise. If it does, the interest—unless it terminates by its own terms earlier—is bound to become invalid under § 1 eventually. There is no point in deferring the right to reformation until the inevitable happens. The Uniform Rule provides for early reformation in such an event, just in case it arises. Consider the following example.

Example 5.22: G devised the residue of his estate in trust, directing the trustee to divide the income, by representation, among *G*'s descendants living from time to time, for 100 years. At the end of the 100 years, the trustee is to distribute the corpus to *G*'s then-living descendants, by representation.

Because the remainder interest in *G*'s descendants living 100 years after *G*'s death can vest but not before 90 years, the Uniform

Rule grants a right to early reformation. The most appropriate form of reformation would be to reduce the 100-year period to 90 years.

§ 5.15   Charitable   Gifts   and Commercial Transactions

This section discusses the application of the Rule Against Perpetuities to charitable gifts and commercial transactions.

Future interests created in charities are subject to the common-law Rule and the Uniform Rule in the same way as future interests created in private parties, with one exception. The exception concerns future interests in a charity that are preceded by an interest created in another charity. In such a case, the future interest in a charity will not be subject to the common-law Rule or the Uniform Rule. Consider the following example.

Example 5.23: G devised land "to the X-School so long as the land is used for school purposes, and upon the cessation of such use, to Y-Church."

The executory interest created in the church is exempt from both the common-law Rule and the Uniform Rule, and is therefore valid.

The rationale for this exemption is that the law allows property to be tied up perpetually for a single charity, so it ought to accord the same treatment to shifts from one charity to another.

It should also be noted that, where this exemption does not apply because the preceding interest is noncharitable, there is a pronounced tendency in the case law to construe the charitable interest as vested if the dispositive language permits that construction. Many charitable interests, otherwise invalid, have been saved by this constructional device.

With respect to commercial transactions, some contracts create property interests that are subject to the common-law Rule. Examples of these interests include options in gross, rights of first refusal, and leases scheduled to commence in the future. At common law, such interests are invalid if they are exercisable beyond a life in being plus 21 years. The perpetuity argument is usually raised by the party seeking to avoid performing on his or her part of the contract.

An *option in gross* is a contract right to purchase property held by an optionee who has no possessory interest in the property. If the subject of an option is land or a unique chattel, the option is specifically enforceable. Specifically enforceable contracts are treated as creating equitable property interests. Since equitable property interests are subject to the common-law Rule, the great majority view at common law is that options in gross are invalid if they are exercisable beyond a life in being plus 21 years.

Example 5.24: (1) A, the owner of Blackacre, sells an option to *B* under which *A* obligates himself and his heirs and assigns to convey Blackacre at any time in the future to *B* and her heirs and assigns, for $X.00.

(2) A, the owner of Blackacre, sells Blackacre to *B*. As part of the transaction, *B* obligates herself and her heirs and assigns to reconvey Blackacre at any time in the future to *A* and his heirs and assigns for $X.00.

The great majority view at common law is that both options are invalid. This means that neither option is specifically enforceable and that damages are not recoverable for its breach.

Note that the option in Variation (2) was reserved by the transferor. Although reversionary interests are not subject to the Rule, reserved options are not granted the same immunity. See *Woodall v. Bruen*, 76 W.Va. 153, 85 S.E. 170 (1915).[9] Yet the difference between a reserved option and a right of entry may only be a matter of form. Suppose the grant in Variation (2) had read "to *B* and her heirs, but if the grantor or his heirs should ever tender $X.00 to *B* or her heirs or assigns, the grantor or his heirs shall have the right to re-enter and retake the premises." Presumably this change in form would transform *A*'s invalid option into a valid right of entry.

Options that expire if they are not exercised within a life in being plus 21 years are valid. The options in the preceding example would have been valid at common law if the owner's obligation to sell had been limited to "the lifetime of the survivor of *A* and *B*," or to "the next 21 years," or to some other period within the Rule. Even if not explicitly so limited, a court might construe the language of the option as being so limited. The absence of language such as "his/her heirs and assigns," for instance, might lead a court to hold that the option was to last only during the lifetime

---

[9]West Virginia subsequently enacted the Uniform Rule, including its exemption of commercial transactions.

of either party or only during their joint lives.

Unlike options to purchase, *rights of first refusal* do not obligate the owner to sell. They only obligate the owner to offer the property first to the preemptioner if the owner decides to sell. The preemptioner can buy or decline. If the preemptioner declines, the owner is then free to sell to anyone else. Rights of first refusal have been held to be subject to the common-law Rule, and void if they are exercisable beyond a life in being plus 21 years. See *Ferrero Const. Co. v. Dennis Rourke Corp.*, 311 Md. 560, 536 A.2d 1137 (1988).

A *lease scheduled to commence in the future* is invalid if it is subject to a contingency that might occur beyond a life in being plus 21 years. There has been considerable litigation concerning so-called "on-completion" leases—leases scheduled to commence when construction of a building is completed. On-completion leases would clearly be valid if the lessor was obligated to complete construction within 21 years, but in the absence of an obligation of this sort, some courts have held the lease to be invalid. See *Southern Airways Co. v. DeKalb County*, 102 Ga.App. 850, 118 S.E.2d 234 (1960)(rev'd on other grounds). Other courts, though, have upheld such leases on the theory that the lessee's interest was vested from the beginning, see *Isen v. Giant Food Inc.*, 295 F.2d 136 (D.C. Cir. 1961), or that there was an implicit obligation to complete the building within a reasonable time, see *Singer Co. v. Makad Inc.*, 213 Kan. 725, 518 P.2d 493 (1974).

In our view, the Rule Against Perpetuities is an inappropriate tool of social policy with respect to such transactions. The period of a life in being plus 21 years makes sense as a limit on donative transfers of property but is unsuitable for bargained-for exchanges. Agreeing with this perspective, the Uniform Rule provides in § 4(1) that all commercial transactions are excluded from the Rule. Another approach taken by some states is to enact statutory provisions limiting the duration of certain commercial transactions to a flat number of years. See 765 Ill. Comp. Stat. 305/4; Mass. Gen. Laws ch. 184A, § 5.

§ 5.16   Dynasty Trusts

Restated in 1986, but scheduled to be repealed in 2010, the federal generation-skipping transfer tax (GSTT) has spurred a growing movement for states to abolish the Rule Against Perpetuities. A few states had already abolished the Rule before

1986—including Wisconsin, South Dakota, and Idaho—but the number of states abolishing the Rule in the years after 1986 has grown rapidly. Why is this so, given that the GSTT imposes high taxes on trusts that persist through more than one generation? The answer is that the GSTT also contains a large exemption—over $1 million per donor, and over $2 million for married donors acting together. This exemption relies only on state perpetuity law to control the length of exempt trusts. Furthermore, despite the growing movement to abolish the Rule, Congress continues to rely on state perpetuity law to control the length of exempt trusts. Indeed, not only has Congress allowed the GSTT exemption to remain in existence despite the Rule abolition movement, but Congress recently increased the amount of the exemption to reflect inflation. Previously, the exemption amount was fixed at $1 million, but beginning in 1999 the amount rose in increments of $10,000 as inflation increased, and beginning in 2004 the amount is equal to the estate tax exclusion amount. See Internal Revenue Code § 2631(c). Because of the commercial interests of banks and local attorneys, states are beginning to compete with one another for true dynasty trusts—trusts that last perpetually (or as long as the settlor wants), not for a mere ninety years or for the length of lives in being plus 21 years. For important study of this phenomenon, see Robert H. Sitkoff & Max Schanzenbach, Jurisdictional Competition for Trust Funds: An Empirical Analysis of Perpetuities and Taxes, 115 Yale L.J. (2005).

States jumping on the dynasty trust bandwagon fall into two broad groups. States in the first group have abolished the Rule Against Perpetuities entirely. Other than Wisconsin, South Dakota, and Idaho, already mentioned, this group also includes New Jersey and Rhode Island. States in the second group have made the Rule Against Perpetuities optional, meaning that the settlor may choose to establish a trust not governed by the Rule. Examples here include Arizona, Colorado, Illinois, Maine, Maryland, Missouri, Nebraska, New Hampshire, Ohio, and Virginia.[10] In all of these states except Virginia, the trust must provide some mechanism for the sale or distribution of assets.

In addition, six states have taken idiosyncratic approaches to dynasty trusts. Delaware abolished

[10]The Virginia statute seems designed to be limited to personal property in trust, but as written it applies to "any trust." Va. Code § 55-13.3(C).

the Rule with respect to personal property in trust; real property in trust is subject to a 110-year period of wait-and-see. Nevada and Washington extended the wait-and-see period to 150 years, while Florida and Utah extended it to 360 years and 1,000 years respectively. Wyoming has made the rule optional in a limited sense: the trust must provide that the Rule shall not apply; the trust must require termination no later than 1,000 years after the trust's creation; and the election can only apply to the trust's personal property (real property must be governed by the common-law Rule). Finally, Alaska abolished the Rule except with respect to the creation or exercise of certain powers of appointment.[11]

It remains to be seen what effect the repeal of the GSTT, slated to go into effect in 2010, will have on the abolition movement.

Over time, a perpetual trust is likely to turn into an administrative nightmare. Government statistics

[11]The principal purpose of retaining in Alaska some perpetuity rule for powers of appointment was to avoid the so-called "Delaware Tax Trap." See Jonathan Blattmachr & Jeffrey Pennell, Adventures in Generation-Skipping, or How We Learned to Love the "Delaware Tax Trap," 24 Real Prop., Prob. & Tr. J. 75 (1989).

indicate that the average married couple has 2.1 children. Under this assumption, the average settlor will have more than 100 descendants (who are beneficiaries of the trust) 150 years after the trust is created, around 2500 beneficiaries 250 years after the trust is created, and 45,000 beneficiaries 350 years after the trust is created. Five hundred years after the trust is created, the number of living beneficiaries could rise to an astonishing 3.4 million.

CHAPTER 6

THREE OTHER RULES
GOVERNING FUTURE INTERESTS

This chapter covers three rules of future interest law that remain in force in some U.S. states. Law students should be aware of these rules, which remain as traps for the unwary. The rules are: (1) the rule of the destructibility of contingent remainders; (2) the rule in Shelley's Case; and (3) the doctrine of worthier title.

§ 6.1 The Rule of the Destructibility of Contingent Remainders

The *rule of the destructibility of contingent remainders*, known in shorthand as the "destructibility rule," dates from the late sixteenth century. It provides that *a legal contingent remainder (meaning a contingent remainder directly in land rather than in a trust) is destroyed if it does not vest by the time the preceding freehold estate terminates*. The rule does not apply if the preceding estate is nonfreehold, such as a term of years.

The best way to understand the rule is to see it in operation, as in the following example.

> *Example 6.1: G* transferred land "to *A* for life, remainder to *B* if *B* lives to age 21." At *A*'s death, *B* is under 21.

At *A*'s death, *B*'s remainder is still contingent, because we do not yet know whether *B* will live to age 21. Accordingly, *G*'s reversion operates. In a jurisdiction without the destructibility rule, *G*'s reversion vests in possession as a defeasible fee subject to *B*'s interest, now no longer a contingent remainder but instead an executory interest. In a jurisdiction with the destructibility rule, *G*'s reversion vests in possession as a fee simple absolute; *B*'s contingent remainder, instead of becoming an executory interest, is destroyed. Note that this result occurs irrespective of *G*'s intention. The destructibility rule is a mandatory rule of law, not a default rule of construction.

The case of *Purefoy v. Rogers*, 85 Eng. Rep.

1181 (K.B. 1671), presented an opportunity for the common-law courts to save contingent remainders such as *B*'s by declaring that the remainder could change into an executory interest. But this was not to be. The judges in *Purefoy v. Rogers* declared that a contingent remainder cannot avoid destruction by changing into an executory interest:

> [F]or where a contingency is limited to depend on an estate of freehold which is capable of supporting a remainder, it shall never be construed to be an executory devise, but a contingent remainder only, and not otherwise.

The destructibility rule has its origins in the English feudal system before the Statute of Uses. In that system, the transfer of land from one person to another meant the transfer of seisin, or the right to possess the land. In the prototypical transfer with a future interest—*G* transfers land "to *A* for life, remainder to *B*"—seisin would pass initially from *G* to *A*. Under a legal fiction accepted at common law, *A* would hold seisin for herself and for *B*, and at *A*'s death seisin would pass to *B*. But in Example 6.1, *B* has not, at *A*'s death, satisfied the condition precedent to possession and thus would not be capable of accepting seisin, thereby triggering a reversion to *G*. Yet *G* would hold seisin for herself only, because English law did not permit the holder of an interest in fee simple to hold seisin partly on behalf of another. Only the holder of a freehold interest *less* than fee simple (such as a life estate) could do so. Accordingly, *G*'s reversion vesting in possession as a fee simple would give seisin to *G* alone, and *B*'s contingent remainder would be destroyed.

The destructibility rule never applied to executory interests, because the Statute of Uses enabled seisin to shift (or spring) to the holder of such interests even without a preceding freehold estate for support. Put differently: the conceptual and legal structures that gave rise to the destructibility rule were altered by the Statute of Uses, with the result that executory interests were not subject to destruction.

Example 6.1 involved one typical scenario of destructibility: a *gap in time* between the termination of the freehold estate and the vesting of the remainder. There is also a second scenario in which the destructibility rule operated, involving the doctrine of *merger*. The doctrine of merger provides that *if, after creation, a life estate and a successive vested future interest in fee come into the hands of the same person, the life estate terminates by merging into the other interest.* Consider the following example.

> *Example 6.2: (1)* G devised land "to *A* for life, remainder to *B* if *B* survives *A*." *G*'s will contains no residuary clause, and *G*'s sole heir is *R*.
>
> *(2)* G devised land "to *A* for life, remainder to *B* if *B* survives *A*, but if not, to *C*." *G*'s will contains no residuary clause, and *G*'s sole heir is *R*.

In both cases, *R* has a reversion, albeit merely a technical one in Variation (2). If *R* conveys his reversion to *A*, *A*'s life estate will merge into the reversion, giving *A* a fee simple. If the destructibility rule is not in force, the merger would produce a fee simple defeasible, with the contingent remainders in *B* (and in Variation (2), in *C*) changing into executory interests. If the destructibility rule is in force, the merger would destroy the contingent remainders of *B* and *C*, giving *A* a fee simple absolute. Note that the same results would obtain if *A* had initially conveyed his life estate to *R*, rather than the reverse, or if both *A* and *R* had conveyed their interests to a third person.[1]

Whether triggered by time gap or merger,[2] the rule of destructibility was a part of the common law and, as such, was received in American jurisdictions. Today, however, most states have abolished the rule by statute or abrogated it by

---

[1]Suppose instead that *A* was sole heir, not *R*, meaning that at *G*'s death *A* received both the life estate and the reversion. Would they merge at that moment? No. A life estate and reversion created simultaneously in the same person (*A*) do not merge at creation if there is an intervening contingent remainder. But the interests will merge upon a post-creation transfer to a third party. For example, if *A* conveyed the life estate and reversion to a third party, *X*, the interests would merge and the contingent remainders of *B* (and in Variation (2), *C*) would be destroyed.

[2]The destructibility rule could also be triggered in England by *forfeiture*—for example, when a life tenant purported to convey a fee simple. The transferee would receive a "tortious fee," an estate in fee simple that was subject to a right of entry in the person holding the next vested estate, typically the reversioner. The fact that the transferee's estate was an estate in fee simple caused the destruction of any contingent remainder previously supported by the life estate.

Forfeiture of a life estate was never recognized in the United States. The American rule is that a person can convey no greater estate than he has (in Latin, *nemo dat quod non habet*). Thus, a life tenant in the United States can convey no more than a life estate.

judicial decision. In the remaining minority of states, the question is largely open, although the Restatement of Property § 240 takes the position that the rule is not part of American law. Only in Florida can one find post-World War II decisions endorsing the rule. See *In re Estate of Rentz*, 152 So.2d 480 (Fla.App. 1963).

Is the destructibility rule a sound instrument of social policy? There is no doubt that legal contingent future interests hinder the free alienability of land. Contingent future interests are often created in a class that includes unborn or unascertained persons. Thus the destructibility rule might be seen as promoting the free alienability of property by destroying interests that cannot be transferred. One can speculate that this view of the destructibility rule accounted for the decision in *Purefoy v. Rogers*. It was also about this time that the first seeds of the Rule Against Perpetuities began to emerge.

In our view, however, the destructibility rule is a poor instrument of social policy. Its application is narrow (only legal contingent remainders in land following a freehold), hence the rule is easily avoided by careful drafting. In contrast, the Rule Against Perpetuities applies more widely: to executive interests as well as contingent remainders, to equitable interests as well as legal interests, and to personalty as well as to land. True, the Rule Against Perpetuities allows property to be tied up for quite a long time, but there are solutions to the problem of inalienable land other than destructibility. One such solution might be legislation authorizing the life tenant, with court approval, to sell the property in fee simple absolute with the proceeds put in trust, the income going to the life tenant for life, then the corpus on the life tenant's death going to the person entitled thereto. See generally William F. Fratcher, A Modest Proposal for Trimming the Claws of Legal Future Interests, 1972 Duke L.J. 517.

§ 6.2   The Rule in Shelley's Case

The *rule in Shelley's Case* derives its name from the case of *Wolfe v. Shelley*, 1 Co. Rep. 93b, 76 Eng. Rep. 206 (K.B. 1581). The rule itself, however, was recognized at least two centuries earlier. The rule provides that *a remainder interest in land in favor of the life tenant's heirs*[3] *is held by the life tenant.*[4] Consider the following example.

> *Example 6.3: (1) G* transferred land "to *A* for life, remainder to *A*'s heirs."

[3]For purposes of the rule in Shelley's Case, most American jurisdictions interpret this word in its standard sense: the persons who succeed to property if the owner dies intestate. A remainder in the life tenant's heirs so understood triggers the rule. A few American jurisdictions adopt a contrary view, holding that the rule applies only when heirs is understood in a different sense: an indefinite line including not just the first takers in intestacy (heirs in the standard sense) but also their heirs, their heirs' heirs, and so on forever. By way of example, a transfer by *G* "to *A* for life, remainder to *A*'s heirs who are living at *A*'s death" would trigger the rule in most jurisdictions, because the extra wording merely restates the standard definition. But the rule would not be triggered in the jurisdictions requiring a remainder in an indefinite succession of generations, because that is not the remainder this particular grantor (*G*) created.

Even in the majority of jurisdictions, the remainder must be described in a way that is definitionally equal to the life tenant's "heirs." A remainder in the life tenant's "children" will not trigger the rule even if it turns out in fact that the life tenant's children are his only heirs. See Restatement 2d of Property § 30.1 cmt. g.

[4]The rule also applies to remainders in favor of the heirs of the life tenant's body, but this formulation is too rare in modern times to be worth discussing. See also § 2.5 on the status of the fee tail under American law.

(2) G transferred land "to *A* for the life of *X*, remainder to *A*'s heirs."

(3) G transferred land "to *X* for life, then to *A* for life, remainder to *A*'s heirs."

Without the rule in Shelley's Case, *A* has an interest in the property for life, after which the property passes to *A*'s heirs. Applying the rule yields a very different result: *A* holds both an interest for life and the remainder in fee, which in this example is indefeasibly vested. On these facts, the doctrine of merger (explained in § 6.1) would apply, giving *A* the land in fee simple absolute in Variations (1) and (2) and giving *A* a remainder in fee simple absolute in Variation (3). Note that the rule in Shelley's Case does not automatically trigger a merger; it merely gives the remainder interest to the life tenant. Merger occurs only if the independent requirements of the merger doctrine are met.

The application of the rule occurs without regard to what *G* intended when making the transfer. The rule in Shelley's Case is an absolute rule of law, not a rule of construction that yields to an expression of contrary intent. Moreover, the rule governs transfers of land whether made outright or in trust, meaning that both legal and equitable remainders are subject to it.[5] The rule also applies equally to inter vivos and testamentary transfers of land. The rule does not apply to personalty.[6]

The traditional explanation for the rule points to the English feudal system. In that system, land was not devisable by will; instead, it descended to one's heirs at death. If we imagine Example 6.3 within a feudal system, the land would pass to *A*'s heirs no matter whether *A* owned a life estate or the entire property. The crucial distinction comes in the method of transfer. Without the rule, the heirs would take the land by purchase, meaning by the terms of *G*'s disposition; with the rule, the heirs would take by descent, meaning by operation of law. In the latter case, but not in the former, the feudal lord would be able to exact dues from the heirs before allowing them to receive the land.

---

[5] The rule applies only where the life estate and the remainder are of the same quality, meaning that they must both be legal interests or both be equitable interests. If one is legal and the other equitable, the rule does not apply. See Restatement 2d of Property § 30.1(1) & cmt. h.

[6] An apparent exception is Ohio, where in *Society Nat'l Bank v. Jacobson*, 54 Ohio St.3d 15, 560 N.E.2d 217 (1990), the Ohio Supreme Court in a muddled opinion applied the rule in Shelley's Case to personal property in trust.

Thus, the explanation goes, the rule in Shelley's Case protected lords and their revenue from attempts to evade the payment of feudal obligations.

The typical disposition triggering the rule is the one in Example 6.3, Variation (1): a transfer "to *A* for life, remainder to *A*'s heirs." Yet the rule can also be triggered on more complex facts.

Consider, for instance, the problem of fractional interests. Some cases have arisen in which the life estate and the remainder were of an undivided fraction of the whole. Little difficulty arises when the fractions correspond.

Example 6.4: *G* transferred land "to *A* and *B* equally for their respective lives, and on the death of each, *A*'s half to *A*'s heirs and *B*'s half to *B*'s heirs."

The rule in Shelley's case and the doctrine of merger combine to give *A* and *B* each an undivided half of the fee, probably as tenants in common rather than as joint tenants. See Restatement 2d of Property § 30.1 illus. 27.

Even when the fractions do not correspond, the applicability of the rule can still be determined.

Example 6.5: G transferred land "to A for life, remainder in half to B and in the other half to the heirs of A."

The rule in Shelley's case and the doctrine of merger combine to give A an undivided half in fee simple absolute; the other half is held by A for life, with the remainder in that half going to B.

Example 6.6: G transferred land "to A and B equally for life, and on the death of each, to the heirs of A."

A has only a life estate in half, so the rule in Shelley's Case operates only on half of the remainder. The doctrine of merger then gives A a fee simple in that undivided half. The rule in Shelley's Case does not apply to the other undivided half—the half in which B has a life estate. See Restatement of Property § 312 illus. 26

For an analysis of the result if the disposition had instead read "on the death *of the survivor*," see Restatement of Property § 312 cmt. r.

The rule in Shelley's Case can also be triggered by events that occur after the initial transfer, if the rule's requirements are subsequently satisfied and if the subsequent satisfaction comes about automatically in accordance with the terms of the original transfer. This can occur, for instance, if the future interest in the life tenant's heirs is transformed from an executory interest into a remainder, as in the following example.

Example 6.7: G transferred land "to A for life, remainder to B, but if B fails to survive A, to A's heirs." B later died, survived by A.

The rule in Shelley's Case does not apply at the time of the initial transfer, because the future interest in A's heirs is an executory interest, not a remainder. At B's death, the interest becomes a remainder, at which point the rule in Shelley's case would apply, converting the remainder intended for A's heirs into a remainder in A. The doctrine of merger would then give A a fee simple absolute. See Restatement § 312 cmt. q; Restatement 2d of Property § 30.1 cmt. p. But see Simes & Smith on Future Interests § 1562 (arguing against post-creation application).

The rule will *not* be triggered by events other than the automatic application of the terms of the original transfer. For example, the rule will not apply if a life estate created in a third party later comes into the hands of the person whose heirs hold the remainder. See the following example.

Example 6.8: *G* transferred land "to *B* for life, remainder to the heirs of *A*." *B* later assigns her life interest to *A*.

The rule in Shelley's Case does not apply, because the life estate was not originally created in the ancestor (*A*).

The rule in Shelley's Case was abolished in England in 1925. In the United States, the rule has been abolished by statute or abrogated by judicial decision in most jurisdictions. It has also been repudiated by the ALI. See Restatement 3d of Property § 16.2. The rule continues in force in a small number of jurisdictions, especially Arkansas and Delaware, where the rule has been invoked in judicial decisions as recently as the 1980s. See *Smith v. Wright*, 300 Ark. 416, 779 S.W.2d 177 (1989); *Estate of Donovan*, 1983 WL 103280 (Del. Ch. Apr. 14, 1983). It is also worth noting that statutes abolishing the rule are usually not retroactive, hence do not apply to pre-effective-date instruments.

Like the destructibility rule, the rule in Shelley's Case might initially seem an instrument of social policy, promoting the alienability of land by enabling the life tenant to obtain a fee simple absolute. Yet the rule in Shelley's Case operates in an even narrower range than the destructibility rule: only to remainders in the life tenant's heirs. This defect, combined with better solutions to the problem of inalienable land (see § 6.1), mean that the rule in Shelley's Case cannot be justified as an instrument of social policy.

§ 6.3   The Doctrine of Worthier Title

The *doctrine of worthier title* derives from England, where it emerged no later than the sixteenth century, and probably earlier. The doctrine provides that *a future interest*[7] *in the grantor's heirs*[8] *is to be treated as a future interest*

[7] The doctrine originally applied as rule of law to remainders in land. Expanded as a rule of construction, the doctrine applies equally to remainders and executory interests, whether legal or equitable, whether in land or in personalty. This is important, as most modern future interests are created in trusts of personalty.

[8] The divergent notion of an indefinite line of succession (see footnote 3) never crept into the worthier title doctrine. The doctrine is thus triggered by future interests in the

retained by the grantor. Consider the following example.

> *Example 6.9:* G transferred property "to *A* for life, remainder to *G*'s heirs."

By the terms of the transfer, *A* receives an interest for life, after which the property passes to *G*'s heirs. Applying the doctrine, however, the transfer is re-written as "to *A* for life, reversion in *G*." The explanation for the worthier title doctrine is the same as the one traditionally offered for the rule in Shelley's Case: both rules require heirs to take property by descent rather than by the terms of the transfer—title by descent being "worthier" than title by purchase—because only on descent could feudal lords exact the customary dues.

The doctrine was abolished in England in 1833 but continues to exist in a modified form in some

grantor's heirs, understood as the persons who succeed to the grantor's intestate estate. Accordingly, a future interest in the grantor's "next of kin" would trigger the doctrine if that term is definitionally the same as "heirs" under state law, whereas a future interest in the grantor's "children" or "descendants" would not (regardless of whether the grantor's children or descendants actually turn out to be his or her heirs at death).

parts of the United States. In order to understand the doctrine's current contours, it is necessary to recognize that the doctrine has split into two branches. The *testamentary branch* concerns transfers made by will; the *inter vivos branch* applies to transfers made during lifetime.

The doctrine's testamentary branch is virtually extinct in the United States. Of the 31 jurisdictions that have addressed the issue by statute or judicial decision, 30 have rejected it. The one outlier state is Maryland, where the state's highest court noted the testamentary branch in *Donnelly v. Turner*, 60 Md. 81 (1883); but no Maryland court has considered the question since then, so the continued existence of the testamentary branch there is doubtful. Moreover, the Restatement of Property § 314(2) and the Restatement 2d of Property § 30.2(2) have squarely rejected the testamentary branch, as has § 2-710 of the Uniform Probate Code. It is fair to say that the worthier title doctrine's testamentary branch is dead in the United States.

In contrast, the inter vivos branch still exists in some American jurisdictions, although very few. Most of the state statutes abolishing the testamentary branch also abolished the inter vivos branch, a notable exception being the statute in Washington, which preserves the inter vivos branch as a rule of construction under certain circumstances. Wash. Rev. Code § 11.12.185.

This jurisprudential transformation—changing the worthier title doctrine from an inflexible rule of law into a rule of construction that yields to an expression of contrary intention—is strikingly unusual and merits a brief discussion. The transformation was the brainchild of Benjamin Cardozo, who announced it in 1919 in the New York case of *Doctor v. Hughes*, 225 N.Y. 305, 122 N.E. 221 (1919), which became an important precedent. The case involved a conveyance of real property to a trustee, to pay the grantor an annuity of $1,500 for life, and upon his death the corpus of the trust was to go to the grantor's "heirs at law." During the grantor's lifetime, creditors of his daughter sought to reach her interest in the trust, arguing that she (as one of the heirs-apparent) had a property interest in the trust. Judge Cardozo rejected their claim on the ground that the grantor's purported gift to his heirs at law amounted to a reversion in himself, and so his daughter had nothing her creditors could attach. This result could have been reached by applying the doctrine of worthier title as a rule of law. But Judge Cardozo was disinclined to decide the case on such a traditional ground. Noting that the doctrine had been abolished in England, Judge Cardozo wrote:

> We do not say that the ancient rule survives as an absolute prohibition limiting the power of a grantor.... But at least the ancient rule survives to this extent: That, to transform into a remainder what would ordinarily be a reversion, the intention [of the grantor] ... must be clearly expressed.

From this time forward, the courts in New York and many other states viewed the inter-vivos branch of the worthier title doctrine as a rule of construction.

Thirty years after *Doctor v. Hughes*, a second important decision was issued by New York's highest court: *In re Burchell's Estate*, 87 N.E.2d 293 (N.Y. 1949). In that case, Judge Bromley lowered the level of evidence needed to overcome the doctrine as a rule of construction. He wrote:

> While we have not yet adopted a rule, either by statute or judicial construction, under which

language limiting an interest to heirs is unequivocally given its full effect, the presumption which exists from the use of the common-law doctrine as a rule of construction has lost much of its force since *Doctor v. Hughes.* Evidence of intent need not be overwhelming in order to allow the remainder to stand. Whether the rule should be abrogated completely is a matter for the Legislature.

Both of these decisions deserve severe criticism. Shifting a rule of law to a rule of construction, as Judge Cardozo did in *Doctor v. Hughes*, is not a natural evolutionary step in legal development. Rules of law and rules of construction are based on entirely different premises. Rules of law are intent-defeating; rules of construction are intent-effectuating. Defeating intention is only justified to vindicate goals of sound social policy. When the policy reasons that underlie a rule of law disappear, as they have with respect to the worthier title doctrine, the proper course is for the legislature to repeal the rule (as the English legislature did in 1833) or for the courts to abrogate it. Judge Bromley's attempt to weaken the doctrine by lowering the level of evidence needed to overcome it was unwise. Weak presumptions resolve fewer cases, thus increasing the need for litigation. This is precisely what happened in New York. As Professor Richard Powell observed, "no case involving a substantial sum could fairly be regarded as closed until its language and circumstances had been passed upon" by New York's highest court. Richard R. Powell, Cases on Future Interests 88 (3d ed. 1961).

In 1966, the New York legislature overturned the *Doctor* decision by abolishing the doctrine of worthier title even as a rule of construction. Nevertheless, there are a few states, in addition to the previously mentioned Washington, where the inter vivos branch remains alive as a rule of construction. There are also jurisdictions where one can find cases suggesting that the inter vivos branch may still exist as a rule of law. See *Randall v. Marble*, 69 Me. 310 (1879).

In states where it exists, the doctrine of worthier title can cause unexpected estate tax consequences by causing some or all of the future interest's value to be included in the grantor's gross estate. See Internal Revenue Code §§ 2033, 2037. The doctrine has also caused problems with Special Needs Trusts drafted to provide at the settlor's death for payment of Medicaid expenses followed by distribution of any remaining assets to the settlor's heirs.

Like the destructibility rule and the rule in Shelley's Case, the doctrine of worthier title might be viewed as an instrument of social policy, promoting alienability by untying the fetters purportedly imposed on the property by the grantor's original disposition. If the original conveyance was of a legal interest in land, the doctrine enables the grantor subsequently to transfer a fee simple absolute. If the original conveyance was in an irrevocable trust, the doctrine enables the grantor to join with the other beneficiaries in agreeing to the trust's early termination, thereby permitting the property to be transferred free of trust in fee simple absolute.

Nevertheless, the doctrine of worthier title is a poor instrument of policy. It operates in a very narrow range, and its benefits are dwarfed in comparison to the cost of litigation to determine whether the doctrine as a rule of construction has been overridden by the intention of a particular grantor. The court in *Hatch v. Riggs National Bank*, 361 F.2d 559 (D.C. Cir. 1966), persuasively explained why the doctrine should not remain even as a rule of construction:

We see no reason to plunge the District of Columbia into the ranks of those jurisdictions bogged in the morass of exploring, under the modern doctrine of worthier title, 'the almost ephemeral qualities which go to prove the necessary intent.' The alleged benefit of effectuating intent must be balanced against the resulting volume of litigation and the diversity and difficulty of decision.

Both NCCUSL and ALI share this view. The 1990 revisions to the Uniform Probate Code provide in § 2-710:

The doctrine of worthier title is abolished as a rule of law and as a rule of construction. Language in a governing instrument describing the beneficiaries of a disposition as the transferor's "heirs," "heirs at law," "next of kin," "distributees," "relatives," or "family," or language of similar import, does not create or presumptively create a reversionary interest in the transferor.

The Restatement 3d of Property likewise rejects the doctrine of worthier title as a rule of law and as a rule of construction. See Restatement 3d of

Property § 16.3. The doctrine of worthier title does not represent the intentions of the typical transferor, nor can the doctrine be justified on grounds of social policy.

§ 6.4   Concluding Observations

For the states that have not yet abolished these three rules, we hope that their courts or legislatures will do so promptly. See T.P. Gallanis, The Future of Future Interests, 60 Wash. & Lee L. Rev. 513 (2003) (proposing these and other reforms).

The rules discussed in this chapter are obsolete and should disappear from the law, remaining only the province of the historian.[9]

---

[9]Perhaps also the law student. Notwithstanding Parliament's abolition of the rule in Shelley's Case in 1925, Professor Brian Simpson was still required to learn the rule as an Oxford undergraduate in 1952, "since otherwise, it was argued with perverse but compelling logic, we could not understand what precisely had been abolished." A.W.B. Simpson, Leading Cases in the Common Law 41 (1995).

EXERCISES ON PART I

1. Classify the present and future interests created in the following transfers:

a. *G* transferred land "to *A* for life."

b. *G* transferred land "to *A* for 10 years, then to *B*."

c. *G* transferred land "to *A* for 10 years, then to *B* if *B* is then living."

d. *G* transferred land "to *A* for life, then to *B* if *B* survives *A*, but if not, to *C*."

e. *G* transferred land "to *A* for life, then to *B* if *B* survives *A*, but if not, to *C* if *C* survives *A*."

f. *G* transferred land "to *A* for life, then to *B*, but if *B* fails to survive *A*, to *C*." Do the classifications change if *B* dies before *A*?

2. Do any of the following interests violate the Rule Against Perpetuities? If an interest is valid, identify the validating life.

a. *G* transferred land "to *A* for life, then to *A*'s children who reach age 30." *G* was survived by *A* and *A*'s daughter, *D*. At *G*'s death, *D* was 31.

b. *G* transferred land "to *A* for life, then to the first child of *A* who reaches age 30." *G* was survived by *A* and *A*'s daughter, *D*. At *G*'s death, *D* was 3.

c. *G* devised land "to *A* for 25 years, then to my heirs at law."

d. *G* transferred land "to *A* for life, then for life to such of *A*'s children as reach age 30, then to *B*." When does *B*'s remainder vest in possession?

PART II

MARITAL ESTATES

CHAPTER 7

MARITAL ESTATES AT COMMON LAW

The term *marital estates* refers to interests in property that arise as a result of marriage. There were three marital estates at common law: (1) the life estate by and during coverture; (2) dower; and (3) curtesy.

§ 7.1 Life Estate By and During Coverture

The *life estate by and during coverture* was the interest held by a married man in his wife's land as of the date of their marriage. The interest gave the husband the right to possess and administer the land. He could also unilaterally lease or alienate the land for the duration of the marriage, though not after. (An attempt by the husband to convey the land in fee actually conveyed only his marital interest. To convey the fee, the husband and wife would have to act together.) Any rents and profits received from the land during the marriage belonged to the husband absolutely.

The idea behind coverture was that a legal unity existed between husband and wife, making them one person in the eyes of the law. In the words of Blackstone's Commentaries: "[T]he very being or legal existence of the woman is suspended during the marriage, or at least is incorporated and consolidated into that of the husband." 1 Bl. Com. 430 (1765).

Coverture lasted only during the marriage; the husband's death or the spouses' divorce ended the marital unity, at which point the surviving or former wife regained the power to administer and control her own property.

§ 7.2   Dower

Dower was an interest arising in a surviving wife as of the date of her husband's death. The interest was a life estate in one third of the inheritable land held at any time during the marriage by the husband in fee simple or fee tail.

The principal purpose of dower was to provide support for the surviving widow. It may also have represented a recognition of the wife's contributions to the family estate, and perhaps in addition a partial return of the dowry paid on behalf of the bride. See Thompson on Real Property § 21.02(a). We shall see support and contribution as important rationales for the modern elective share, discussed in the next chapter.

During the husband's life, the wife's right to dower was said to be *inchoate*, but it was still a real right in the following sense: the right to dower could not be defeated by an inter vivos conveyance by the husband to a third party, even to a bona fide purchaser for value. The third party would receive the land subject to the wife's right to dower. (The only exception to this rule occurred if the wife had joined in the conveyance or had otherwise relinquished her right to dower in that land.)

Upon the husband's death, the right to dower became *choate* or *consummate* if they remained married at his death and the wife survived him. Just as the husband could not by inter vivos conveyance defeat the wife's right to dower, so too could he not defeat the right by will.

An interesting question arose whether the wife could receive both the land devised to her by her husband's will and the land that was hers for life by dower. The rule developed that the wife could take both, unless the will clearly expressed that its provision for the wife was in lieu of dower, in which event the wife would be required to choose. A clear expression of this principle appears in *Birmingham v. Kirwan*, 2 Sch. & Lefr. 444 (Irish Ch. 1805):

> The general rule is, that a person cannot accept and reject the same instrument.... The principle, then, that the wife cannot have both dower and what is given in lieu of dower, being acknowledged ... the only question in such cases must be, whether the provision alleged to have been given in satisfaction of dower was so given, or not....
>
> As the right to dower is in itself a clear legal right, an intent to exclude that right, by voluntary gift, must be demonstrated either by express words, or by clear and manifest implication. If there was anything ambiguous or doubtful, if the court cannot say that it was clearly the intention to exclude, then the averment that the gift was made in lieu of dower cannot be supported.... [T]he result of all the cases of implied intention seems to be, that the instrument must contain some provision,

inconsistent with the assertion of the right to demand [the dower interest].

§ 7.3 Curtesy

Curtesy was an interest arising in a surviving husband as of the date of his wife's death. The interest was a life estate in all inheritable land held at any time during the marriage by the wife in fee simple or fee tail, or in which the wife had an equitable estate in fee (meaning that the land was held in trust by someone else for the wife's benefit).

Unlike dower, curtesy had an additional requirement: the husband and wife must have had a child born alive during the marriage capable of inheriting the land from its mother.[1]

Upon the child's birth, the husband held an *estate by the curtesy initiate* (akin to the wife's inchoate dower). Upon the wife's death, the husband held an *estate by the curtesy consummate* if they remained

---

[1]Thompson on Real Property § 21.03(c) gives the following example: "[T]he instrument giving the estate to the wife may be so worded as to make the issue of the wife purchasers instead of heirs, so far as the [given] estate is concerned. If so, the husband will not have an estate by curtesy."

married at her death and he survived her. It did not matter whether or not the child survived her.

The purpose of curtesy was not (as one might think) to aid in supporting the marital children. Rather, the purpose seems to have been to maintain the bond between the wife's feudal lord and the husband—a bond created when the husband received his life estate by and during coverture. See Thompson on Real Property § 21.03(b).

§ 7.4 The Common-Law Marital Estates Today

The *life estate by and during coverture* has been abolished. Women today administer their own property whether or not they are married.

The estates of *dower and curtesy* have been largely abolished. Only a small number of states retain either of these interests.

In place of dower and curtesy, American states provide three layers of protection for a surviving spouse: (1) *statutes of intestate succession*, known formally as *statutes of descent and distribution*, giving the surviving spouse a share of the decedent spouse's intestate estate, (2) statutes authorizing the surviving spouse to take an *elective share* or *forced share* of the decedent spouse's property, and (3) in some states, statutes protecting *omitted spouses* from unrevised premarital wills. There are also states with regimes of *community property*, a concept derived from continental Europe, in which spouses share the assets acquired during marriage. We consider each of these modern protections in the next chapter.

CHAPTER 8

MODERN PROTECTIONS FOR THE SURVIVING SPOUSE

§ 8.1 Introduction

Most jurisdictions in the United States follow the *separate property (or title-based)* system of property ownership that emerged after the elimination of coverture from the common law. Under this system, the husband and wife are separate owners of assets that each person acquires, whether before or during the marriage—except, of course, for items the spouses have agreed to hold jointly. (On concurrent ownership, see Part III.)

One danger of the separate property system is that when the first spouse dies, the surviving spouse may be left penniless. This danger was prevented at common law by the estates of dower and curtesy. In place of the marital estates, most common-law jurisdictions provide two layers of statutory protection for a surviving spouse: (1) statutes of intestate succession, known formally as statutes of descent and distribution, giving the surviving spouse a share of the decedent spouse's intestate estate; and (2) statutes authorizing the surviving spouse to take an elective share of the decedent spouse's property. Some common-law jurisdictions also provide a third layer: protection against inadvertent omission from a premarital will.

§ 8.2   Statutes of Descent and Distribution

A person dying without a valid will has died *intestate*. (When the will does not dispose of all of the decedent's probate property, typically because the will was badly drafted, it is said that the person died *partially intestate*.)

Whether a person dies partially or fully intestate, intestate property is distributed in accordance with intestate succession statutes, known as *statutes of descent and distribution*. This term requires a historical explanation. American statutes on intestate succession are derived from two sources: the common-law canons of descent, which determined inheritance of land; and the English

Statute of Distribution 1670, which governed succession to personal property. Modern American statutes cover both land and personalty, and are called statutes of descent and distribution.

All American statutes of descent and distribution give some share of the decedent's intestate property to his or her surviving spouse. (The term "surviving spouse" indicates that the marriage existed at the decedent's death and that the spouse survived the decedent.)

The traditional approach under American law was to give the surviving spouse a fixed fraction of the decedent's intestate estate, commonly one third or one half, fractions derived from common-law dower and the English Statute of Distribution. The fractions might be larger if the decedent had no surviving descendants. Writing in 1953, Professor Thomas Atkinson described the "typical American position" as giving "the spouse half the estate if issue survives; the first $5000 and half the remainder if there is no issue, and parents or their issue survive; the entire estate in other cases." Thomas E. Atkinson, Handbook of the Law of Wills 63 (2d ed. 1953).

A recent trend in American law has been to

increase even further the intestate share of the surviving spouse. See Restatement 3d of Property § 2.2. At the forefront of this trend is the Uniform Probate Code, which provides in § 2-102, as revised in 1990, that the surviving spouse should receive the entire intestate estate even in the presence of surviving descendants if two conditions are met. The first condition is that the decedent's descendants must also be the descendants of the surviving spouse. The second is that the surviving spouse must have no descendants who are not the decedent's descendants. See UPC § 2-102(1)(ii).

Example 8.1: G died intestate, survived by his spouse, S, and their two children, X and Y.

Under a statute of the type described by Professor Atkinson, S inherits one half of G's estate. X and Y share the other half equally.

Under the Uniform Probate Code, S inherits G's entire estate.

The move to have the spouse inherit the entire estate despite the presence of children is aligned with statutory reforms throughout the United States, Canada, and Europe. Professor Mary Ann Glendon calls this trend the "shrinking circle of heirs" phenomenon. Mary Ann Glendon, The Transformation of Family Law 238 (1989). By this she means that, over time, "the position of the surviving spouse has steadily improved everywhere at the expense of the decedent's blood relatives."

What explains this phenomenon? The answer is that the aim of intestacy law is to mirror what most decedents would wish if they had thought about it (and had taken the time to execute wills). Marriage increasingly is viewed as the most important family relationship, and decedents accordingly want the bulk if not all of their property to pass to the surviving spouse.

This emphasis on the spouse might appear to prejudice the decedent's children. But UPC § 2-102 is based on the insight that the children are not truly losing. The surviving spouse in fact occupies two roles—one as the decedent's primary beneficiary and one as a conduit through whom to benefit the couple's children.

The theory becomes problematic, of course, when some of the children are not joint. If some of the decedent's descendants are not descendants of the surviving spouse, or vice versa, the likelihood decreases that the spouse will serve as a proper conduit. The UPC responds to this problem by awarding the spouse less than the entire intestate estate in such circumstances. See § 2-102(3), (4).

Example 8.2: (1) G died intestate, survived by his spouse, *S*, and his child, *X*, who is not a child of *S*.

(2) G died intestate, survived by his spouse, *S*, their joint child, *Y*, and *S*'s child, *Z*, who is not a child of *G*.

In both Variations, the Uniform Probate Code awards *S* less than the entire estate. *S* receives the first $100,000 plus one half of the balance of the estate in Variation (1), the first $150,000 plus one half of the estate in Variation (2). See UPC § 2-103(3), (4).

§ 8.3   The Elective Share

Most decedents who execute wills and other estate planning documents provide well for their surviving spouses. Some decedents, however, intentionally attempt to disinherit their surviving spouses, or to provide for them only minimally. This is not permitted under modern law.

All but one of the separate-property states[1] have decided that disinheritance of the surviving spouse at death is one of the few instances in which the decedent's testamentary freedom with respect to his or her title-based ownership interests must be curtailed. No matter what the decedent's intent, the separate-property states recognize that the surviving spouse has a claim to a portion of the decedent's estate. These statutes provide the spouse a so-called *forced share*. Because the forced share is expressed as an option that the survivor can elect or let lapse during the administration of the decedent's estate, the better and more descriptive term is an *elective share*.

Under traditional elective-share law, the surviving spouse is entitled to a one-third share of the decedent's probate estate. The term "probate estate" refers to assets that pass under the direction

---

[1]Georgia is the only separate-property state lacking an elective-share statute. For a discussion of the reasons for Georgia's position, including its unusual "year's support" practice, and an argument that elective-share statutes are generally unnecessary, see Verner F. Chaffin, A Reappraisal of the Wealth Transmission Process: The Surviving Spouse, Year's Support and Intestate Succession, 10 Ga. L. Rev. 447 (1976). For an opposing view, see Note, Preventing Spousal Disinheritance in Georgia, 19 Ga. L. Rev. 427 (1985).

of the decedent's will or, in the absence of an effective will, in accordance with the provisions of the statute of descent and distribution. The term does not include assets owned or owned in substance by the decedent that pass outside the probate court's jurisdiction, such as pension or life-insurance proceeds distributed according to a beneficiary designation on file with the decedent's employer or life insurer, assets held in a revocable trust distributed according to the trust's terms, or assets (such as a joint bank account) held by the decedent and another person as joint owners with an automatic right of survivorship.

The traditional law of the elective share provides inadequate protection for the surviving spouse, in two respects. First, the limitation to the probate estate enables the decedent to evade the surviving spouse's entitlement; the decedent can readily place his or her wealth in vehicles such as revocable trusts and joint accounts that pass outside probate.[2] Second, the fixed fraction

---

[2]Courts occasionally hold such transfers fraudulent or illusory, hence still subject to the elective share. See *Newman v. Dore*, 275 N.Y. 371, 9 N.E.2d 966 (1937); *Sullivan v. Burkin*, 390 Mass. 864, 460 N.E.2d 572 (1984). The better remedy is a statute, such as the Uniform Probate Code,

(usually one third) is not responsive to the length of the marriage, which is the period of time during which the couple will have accumulated assets together; it is on these assets that the surviving spouse has a moral claim that should be actualized in law. For discussion, see Restatement 3d of Property §§ 9.1, 9.2.

> *Example 8.3: (1) G* and *S* were married for 1 year. Then *G* died with a will leaving "all my property to X-Charity." *G*'s probate estate was worth $3 million.
>
> *(2) G* and *S* were married for 50 years, then *G* died with a will leaving "all my property to X-Charity." *G*'s probate estate was worth $3,000, but *G* also owned an insurance policy worth $3 million naming his mistress, *M*, as the beneficiary.
>
> Under the traditional elective share, *S* is entitled to $1 million in Variation (1) and $1,000 in Variation (2).

Newer elective-share statutes, such as the Uniform Probate Code, address both of these

---

expressly including nonprobate transfers within the elective share.

deficiencies. First, the UPC reaches beyond the probate estate to a broad range of assets owned or owned in substance by the decedent, including assets passing outside probate. See UPC § 2-205. Second, the UPC entitles the surviving spouse to a sliding percentage of the couple's combined property. Depending on the facts, this might be less or more than the traditional one third. A marriage lasting at least one year but less than two years yields an elective share percentage of 3 percent. A marriage of fifteen years or more yields an elective share percentage of 50 percent. See UPC § 2-202(a).[3]

§ 8.4   Inadvertent Omission from Premarital Will

Nearly all American jurisdictions have statutes, called "pretermitted heir" statutes, that grant the decedent's children a measure of protection from being inadvertently disinherited. The statutes typically apply when the decedent's will was executed before the child was born or adopted.

---

[3]The UPC also provides for a supplemental share, where needed, to bring the spouse's assets plus the spouse's elective share to $50,000. See UPC § 2-202(b).

Similar protection for the surviving spouse is uncommon, although some states provide it. See Restatement 3d of Property § 9.5. The protection is particularly evident in those states adopting § 2-301 of the Uniform Probate Code. As revised in 1990, the section provides that if the decedent executed the will before the marriage, the surviving spouse is entitled to receive a share of the decedent's probate estate, unless (1) it appears that the will was made in contemplation of the marriage, (2) the will expresses the intention to omit the future spouse, or (3) the decedent provided for the spouse outside the will and there is evidence that such provision was intended to be in lieu of a share of the will.

If this rule entitles the spouse to a share, there is still the matter of computing the share. The UPC section in its current form provides that the share is to be the amount the spouse would have received if the decedent had died intestate as to that portion of the estate not devised to a descendant of the decedent (but not of the surviving spouse) born before the marriage, or passing to such a person's descendants under an antilapse statute. This may seem a bit complicated, but it is illustrated in the following examples.

Example 8.4: G and *S-1* were married for thirty years. After *S-1* died, G married *S-2*. G died with a will executed while *S-1* was alive, giving "all my property to *S-1*, if *S-1* survives me, and if not, to X-Charity."

In most non-UPC jurisdictions, G's property passes to X-Charity.

Under the UPC, *S-2* is entitled to the property *S-2* would have received if G had died intestate as to the portion of G's estate not passing to a descendant of G. On these facts, nothing is passing to such a descendant, so *S-2* is entitled to G's entire estate.

Example 8.5: G and *S-1* were married for thirty years and had a child, C. After *S-1* died, G married *S-2*. G died with a will executed while *S-1* was alive, giving "all my property to *S-1*, if *S-1* survives me, and if not, to C if C survives me, and if not, to X-Charity." G was survived by *S-2* and C.

In most non-UPC jurisdictions and also under the UPC, G's estate passes to C.

The animating principle behind the Uniform Probate Code's protection of the omitted spouse—and its withdrawal of the protection in certain circumstances, particularly where there are devises to children or descendants from a prior relationship—is that these results are the ones the testator would want if he or she had taken the trouble to execute a new will.

§ 8.5   Community Property

So far, we have been speaking of the separate property or title-based system of property ownership, which is derived from English common law and is today followed by most jurisdictions in the United States. There is an alternative. The system known as *community property* developed in continental Europe and was transplanted to the new world by French and Spanish settlers. In a community property system, the husband and wife own all assets acquired by either of them during the marriage in equal undivided shares. The particular community property model appearing in this country is derived from the *community of acquests* concept of the Spanish legal system, under which each spouse owns a half interest in the earnings of the other acquired during the marriage, in effect as a tenant in common (on this term, see § 9.2);[4] property acquired prior to the marriage and property acquired during the marriage by gift or inheritance are not counted in the community, and so remain separate property. The other community property model, called universal community, has not appeared in this country. In universal community systems, each spouse owns a half interest in all the property of the other, regardless of the property's source or time of acquisition.

Nine states (Arizona, California, Idaho, Louisiana, Nevada, New Mexico, Texas,

[4]Because both spouses own community property, problems arise concerning management of community assets. Community property states have statutes prescribing who has power to manage and deal with the assets. These statutes vary considerably, but some generalizations are possible. In Texas, the wife has sole management power over her earnings that are kept separate, and the husband has sole management power over his. In California and several other community property states, either spouse has power, acting alone, to manage community assets. Both spouses, however, ordinarily are required to join in transfers or mortgages of community real property. If one spouse makes a gift of community property to a third party, the non-donor spouse may set it aside entirely or in excess of a stated amount. See J. Thomas Oldham, Management of the Community Estate During an Intact Marriage, 56 L. & Contemp. Prob. 99 (1993).

Washington, and Wisconsin[5]) are community property states. Alaska is an optional community property state, meaning that married persons may choose to classify some or all of their assets as community property.[6]

Interest in community property has been growing, thanks to an emerging consensus in favor of economic equalization between husbands and wives. The idea that both marital partners should share equally acquests from the economic activity of either led to the promulgation in 1983 of the

[5]Wisconsin's enactment of the Model Marital Property Act made it a community property state. The Wisconsin legislature, however, modified the MMPA in several respects. See Howard S. Erlanger & June M. Weisberger, From Common Law Property to Community Property: Wisconsin's Marital Property Act Four Years Later, 1990 Wis. L. Rev. 769 (1990).

[6]For discussion, see Jonathan G. Blattmachr, Howard M. Zaritsky & Mark L. Ascher, Tax Planning with Consensual Community Property: Alaska's New Community Property Law, 33 Real Prop., Prob. & Tr. J. 615 (1999). The Alaska Community Property Act, effective May 23, 1998, also permits residents and non-residents to establish community property trusts, holding specific assets as community property. See Jonathan G. Blattmachr & Howard M. Zaritsky, Alaska Consensual Community Property Law and Property Trust, Tr. & Est. 65 (Nov. 1998).

Uniform Marital Property Act, now called the Model Marital Property Act. The MMPA adopts a version of the community of acquests, although the terminology is different: community property is called "marital property" and separate property is called "individual property." Under the MMPA, as under community property, the property interest that each spouse acquires in all the assets acquired by the economic activities of either during the marriage is a present, vested ownership right that does not depend on survival of the other spouse.[7]

----

[7]Under community property systems and the MMPA, the couple's property must be classified upon the first spouse's death, and this in turn sometimes requires tracing the property to its source. To help resolve disputes, these systems recognize a presumption that all property is community or marital property. The spouse alleging that an item is separate or individual property must be able to prove it, and this can be a difficult task as assets over time in a marriage are commingled, invested, reinvested, exchanged and consumed. To resolve classification problems, courts have developed numerous rules applicable to particular types of transactions.

Problems also arise because a couple has moved from a separate property state to a community property state, or the reverse. The basic principle is that the law of the state where the couple was domiciled at the time an asset was acquired controls ownership of the asset.

Detailed consideration of these questions is beyond the scope of this *Nutshell*.

A unique feature of community property regimes is that the surviving spouse is not seen as needing an elective share to protect against disinheritance. The survivor already owns a half interest in the fruits of the marriage. The survivor's contribution having been rewarded, the decedent can be allowed unfettered power of disposition over his or her separate property and his or her portion of the community property.[8]

> *Example 8.6:* G and S, married for fifty years, hold all their assets as community property. G died with a will leaving "all my property to X-Charity."
>
> G is entitled to dispose of one half of the community. S retains one half. No elective share is needed to prevent disinheritance.

[8] In practice, decedents often wish to benefit their surviving spouses. California permits spouses to create "community property with right of survivorship," which passes automatically to the survivor as if in joint tenancy. See Cal. Civ. Code § 682.1.

PART III

CONCURRENT ESTATES

CHAPTER 9

CONCURRENT ESTATES

§ 9.1 Introduction

Anglo-American law permits multiple persons to hold the same interests in the same property. Because these interests are held concurrently, rather than successively, they are known as *concurrent estates*.

Consider the following example.

Example 9.1: G transferred land "to *A* and *B* and their heirs."[1]

---

[1] In the remaining examples in this chapter, the words of limitation "and their heirs" will be omitted, as unnecessary to create interests in fee simple absolute. (Recall § 2.3.)

215

A and *B* each hold a fee simple absolute. Their interests are concurrent, not successive.

Three concurrent estates exist today: (1) joint tenancy, (2) tenancy in common, and (3) tenancy by the entirety. The fourth—tenancy in coparcenary—no longer exists.

§ 9.2   The Tenancies Defined

Joint tenancy[2] is a concurrent estate held by multiple persons who share what are traditionally called the *four unities*:

(1) *unity of time*: the persons receive their interests in the property at the same moment;

(2) *unity of title*: the persons receive their interests from the same source, meaning the same deed or will;

(3) *unity of interest*: the persons receive the same type of interest, e.g., a fee simple or a life estate; and

(4) *unity of possession*: each person has the same right to possess the property.

---

[2]This material refers primarily to joint tenancies in land. On the joint bank account, see § 9.8.

The main feature of a joint tenancy is that the joint tenants have a *right of survivorship*. When one joint tenant dies, his or her interest in the property automatically passes to the other joint tenants. The interest does not pass to the decedent's devisees or heirs.

> *Example 9.2:* G transferred land "to *A* and *B* as joint tenants and not as tenants in common." Later, *A* died with a will devising "all my property to my niece, *N*." *A*'s heir at law was his son, *S*. *A* was survived by *B*, *N*, and *S*.
>
> *A*'s interest in the land passes automatically at *A*'s death to *B*. It does not pass to *N* or *S*.

Joint tenancies are recognized in most American jurisdictions, but not all. Some states have abolished the joint tenancy. For example, Alaska has abolished joint tenancies in land, and Oregon has re-labeled the joint tenancy as "tenancy in common in the life estate with cross-contingent remainders in the fee simple." See Alaska Stat. § 34.15.130; Or. Rev. Stat. § 93.180. Some other states recognize the joint tenancy but not its right of survivorship. See Ark. Code § 28-8-101; Fla. Stat. § 689.15; Tenn. Code § 66-1-107.

On the current preference for tenancy in common, see § 9.3.

Tenancy in common is a concurrent estate requiring only one unity: the *unity of possession*, meaning that each tenant in common has the same right to possess the property. Tenancy in common does not have the survivorship feature of joint tenancy. When one tenant in common dies, his or her interest passes to his or her devisees or heirs, not to the other tenants in common.

> *Example 9.3: G* transferred land "to *A* and *B* as tenants in common." Later, *A* died with a will devising "all my property to my niece, *N*." *A*'s heir at law was his son, *S*. *A* was survived by *B*, *N*, and *S*.
>
> *A*'s interest in the land passes by will to *N*. There is no right of survivorship between *A* and *B*.

Tenancy by the entirety is a special form of joint tenancy existing only between husband and wife. At common law, it was said that tenancy by the entirety required five unities: the four unities of joint tenancy plus a fifth unity—*unity of person*. (Recall the common law view that husband and wife were one person; see § 7.1.) Like joint tenancy, tenancy by the entirety includes an automatic right of survivorship.

> *Example 9.4:* G transferred land "to A and B, husband and wife, as tenants by the entirety." Later, A died with a will devising "all my property to my niece, N." A's heirs at law were his wife, B, and his son, S. A was survived by B, N, and S.
>
> A's interest in the land passes automatically at A's death to B. It does not pass to N or S.

Today, a majority of American jurisdictions have abolished the tenancy by the entirety; these states recognize only the joint tenancy and the tenancy in common.

Tenancy in coparcenary was the concurrent estate created at common law when land was inherited by two or more persons (in contrast to the typical practice, primogeniture, which involved inheritance by one heir, the eldest male).

> *Example 9.5:* G transferred land "to A and his heirs." Later, A died without a will, survived by his daughters, X and Y, who were his heirs.

A's interest in the land passes by descent to *X* and *Y* as coparceners.

American jurisdictions never recognized this tenancy. Instead, the concurrent estates created when a decedent dies intestate survived by multiple heirs are generally tenancies in common. This is true even though some statutes use the terminology of the tenancy in coparcenary. See Thompson on Real Property §§ 31.01, 35.08.

§ 9.3   The Creation of Concurrent Estates

At common law, joint tenancy was the preferred form of concurrent ownership. A transfer of property by deed or will to "*A* and *B* and their heirs" created a joint tenancy.[3]

Modern statutes and judicial decisions, however, prefer the tenancy in common. In the majority of states, the current law presumes that a transfer to multiple persons creates a tenancy in common unless the transferor manifests an intention to

---

[3]Unless *A* and *B* were husband and wife, in which case the transfer created a tenancy by the entirety.

create a joint tenancy.[4]

The rationale for the modern approach seems to be that the recipients of property should not enjoy an automatic right of survivorship unless the transferor has evidenced the intention to create the right. There has been much litigation on whether a particular transferor has or has not provided sufficient evidence of intention. Consider the following example.

Example 9.6: G transferred land "to *A* and *B* jointly."

In states with a presumption in favor of tenancy in common, the lone word "jointly" will typically be insufficient to overcome the presumption; *A* and *B* will take as tenants in common. In a few states, however, the statute creating the presumption expressly allows the presumption to be rebutted by the word

---

[4]Among the states recognizing the tenancy by the entirety, there is a split of authority on whether a transfer to spouses is presumed to create a tenancy by the entirety, on the one hand, or a tenancy in common or joint tenancy, on the other. There is also a split of authority on the effect of a transfer to unmarried persons "as tenants by the entirety." Some jurisdictions treat this as a joint tenancy, others as a tenancy in common.

"jointly"; in which case, *A* and *B* will take as joint tenants. See Thompson on Real Property §31.06(d).

Another much litigated question concerns the ability of a transferor to create a joint tenancy by conveying the property to himself and another. At common law, this did not satisfy the required unities of time and title—each joint tenant must receive the interest from the same document at the same time. Accordingly, the practice developed of using a middleman: *G* would convey the land to *X* who would convey it to *G* and *A* as joint tenants. In the majority of states, this two-step procedure is no longer necessary; substance prevails over form, and a transferor may convey property to himself and one or more third parties as joint tenants.

Example 9.7: *G* transferred land "to *G* and *A* as joint tenants."

In the majority of states, this transfer suffices to create a joint tenancy. *G* and *A* hold as joint tenants, i.e. with an automatic right of survivorship between them.

A similar rule prevails in the states recognizing the tenancy by the entirety: one spouse may convey to both spouses as tenants by the entirety, as in the following example.

Example 9.8: G transferred land "to *G* and *A*, husband and wife, as tenants by the entirety."

This transfer is sufficient to create a tenancy by the entirety in most of the states recognizing the tenancy.

§ 9.4   Relations Among Concurrent Tenants

As we have seen in § 9.2, the holders of any concurrent estate enjoy unity of possession, meaning the same right to possess and enjoy the whole property. This means that a cotenant in exclusive possession does not owe rent to the other cotenants.

Example 9.9: G transferred land "to *A* and *B*" as tenants in common or as joint tenants (in this example, it makes no difference). *A* is occupying the land; *B* lives elsewhere.

A has the right to possess and enjoy the entire land. *A* does not owe rent to *B*. Nor, without more, is *A*'s sole occupancy adverse to *B* for purposes of adverse possession.

Conversely, no cotenant has the right to exclude the other cotenants. Such exclusion would be an impermissible ouster, enabling the ousted cotenant to maintain an action to regain possession (and an appropriate share of any profits). Indeed, if the ousted cotenant did not bring an action, he or she could eventually lose title via the doctrine of adverse possession.

It frequently happens that not all cotenants are in possession at any given time. It is worth repeating that this by itself is not an ouster (and would not lead to title by adverse possession), because each cotenant has the right to possess the whole.

When not all cotenants are in possession, questions arise about the rights and obligations of the cotenants in possession with respect to those who are not.

The background rule at common law is that the cotenants in possession may treat the property as their own. There are two important limitations to this rule, however. First, the Statute of Anne 1704, as interpreted by the English judges, requires the cotenants in possession to account to the other cotenants for any rents received from a third person.

Example 9.10: G transferred land "to A and B" as cotenants. A occupies the land; B lives elsewhere. A rents a room on the land to X at the rate of $1,000 per month.

B is entitled to $500 per month from A. If A refuses to pay it, B may bring an action of account against A to force payment.

Most American jurisdictions follow this English statute, either by legislation or by declaring it to be part of their common law, and some extend it to other forms of income and profits generated by the cotenant in possession himself.

Example 9.11: G transferred land "to A and B" as cotenants. A occupies the land; B lives elsewhere. A removed and sold minerals from the land, earning a net profit of $10,000.

In some jurisdictions, the duty to account (rather than the duty to avoid waste, see below) applies to these facts, meaning that B is entitled to a pro rata share of the net profits, in this instance $5,000. If A refuses to pay it, B may bring an action of account to force payment. See *White v. Smyth*, 147 Tex. 272, 214 S.W.2d 967 (1948).

Second, the cotenants in possession may not permit or cause the property to suffer permanent damage ("waste"). What constitutes waste varies widely from one jurisdiction to another, and even when damage such as cutting timber or removing minerals is labeled waste, the typical remedy is simply the same as we have already observed for rents and profits: an accounting to the other cotenants for the net profits received. Rarely is the traditional English penalty for waste—treble damages—imposed against cotenants by American courts.

If the cotenants in possession spend money on the property without the consent (express or implied) of the cotenants not in possession, the extent to which the former may require contribution from the latter depends on whether the expenditures were for necessary repairs or for improvements. If for improvements, the widespread rule is that no contribution is required.[5] If for necessary repairs, American jurisdictions are split. Some permit contribution if consent was

---

[5]While the cotenancy exists. In an action for partition (on which see § 9.5), the cotenants in possession can obtain contribution as a part of the final accounting, if the improvements increased the value of the land.

requested, on the theory that the expenditures were necessary and the withholding of consent was unreasonable; others do not because no consent was obtained.

If a cotenant pays more than his or her share of an obligation imposed by law or by agreement—e.g., taxes or a mortgage—he or she is of course entitled to contribution from the other cotenants.

Example 9.12: G transferred land "to A and B" as cotenants. A occupies the land; B lives elsewhere. A paid property taxes of $2,000, spent $500 mending a leaky roof, and spent $5,000 on fancy landscaping.

A is entitled to contribution from B in the amount of $1,000 for the property taxes, and in some jurisdictions (if consent was sought but not obtained) to contribution in the amount of $250 for the roof repair. A is not entitled to contribution for the landscaping.[6]

---

[6]Except perhaps in the final accounting accompanying an action for partition, if the landscaping increases the value of the property. See the previous footnote.

§ 9.5   The Termination of Concurrent Estates

The methods of terminating a concurrent estate vary according to the nature of the estate.

Tenancies in common can be terminated by a *voluntary partition* initiated by all cotenants and effected by an exchange of deeds among them; or if the cotenants cannot agree, any one of them can bring an *action for partition*. Either way, the result of the successful partition is to destroy the unity of possession, subdividing the property into separate parcels each owned by one of the former cotenants. This is called *partition in kind*.

> *Example 9.13:* G transferred unimproved land "to *A* and *B* as tenants in common." Later, *A* brought an action for partition.
>
> The result of the partition is that the land is divided into two parcels, one owned by *A*, the other owned by *B*.

If physical division is impractical—e.g., because the property contains indivisible improvements, such as a house—the proper course is *partition by sale* (again, voluntarily or by court action), whereby the property is sold and the proceeds divided among the former cotenants.

Example 9.14: G transferred land containing a single-family home "to *A* and *B* as tenants in common." *A* occupies the home; *B* lives elsewhere. *A* later brings an action for partition.

The result of the action will be partition by sale, with the proceeds divided between *A* and *B*. Note that *A* (or *B*) might be the purchaser at the sale.

Joint tenancies are also subject to partition in kind or by sale. Short of partition, a joint tenancy can be transformed into a tenancy in common by severing the joint tenancy—in other words, by destroying one or more (but not all) of the four unities. This typically results from a conveyance by a joint tenant to a third party. Consider the following example.

Example 9.15: G transferred land "to *A*, *B*, and *C* as joint tenants and not as tenants in common." Later, *A* conveyed her interest in the land to *X*. Still later, *X* died intestate survived by his sole heir, *H*. Then *B* died.

The conveyance from *A* to *X* severs the joint tenancy (and the right of survivorship) between *A* and *B* and between *A* and *C*. After the conveyance, *X* holds the land as a tenant in common with *B* and *C*, who hold as joint tenants with each other. On *X*'s death, *X*'s interest passes to his heir, *H*. Because *B* and *C* hold the land as joint tenants with each other, when *B* dies before *C*, *B*'s one-third interest passes automatically to *C*. *C* and *H* then hold unequal shares as tenants in common.

The cases are divided on whether the conveyance must be to a third party. (Recall the discussion of the middleman in § 9.3.) Some jurisdictions permit a joint tenancy to be severed, hence transformed into a tenancy in common, by a joint tenant transferring his interest to himself. See *Riddle v. Harmon*, 102 Cal.App.3d 524 (1980).

Example 9.16: *G* transferred land "to *A* and *B* as joint tenants and not as tenants in common." Later, *A* transferred his interest in the land "to *A* as tenant in common."

In some jurisdictions, the transfer is effective to sever the joint tenancy, transforming it into a tenancy in common, hence without a right of survivorship between *A* and *B*.

There is also uncertainty about whether actions short of a conveyance will be sufficient to trigger a severance of the joint tenancy. Some cases and authorities state that a mortgage or lease of one joint tenant's interest will be sufficient; others take the opposite view. Am. L. Prop. § 6.2; Thompson on Real Property § 31.08(b).

The *tenancy by the entirety* is subject to partition, but only if both spouses agree. The agreement of both spouses is also generally needed to convey an interest to a third party. Absent partition, a tenancy by the entirety will terminate only on death or divorce. In the latter event, jurisdictions are divided on whether the former spouses—if they continue to hold concurrent estates—are tenants in common or joint tenants.

§ 9.6 Creditors' Rights

An overarching principle governing the rights of creditors in concurrent estates is that the creditor can have no greater rights than the debtor. Hence, the following material is largely an application of the principles discussed in § 9.5.

The creditor of a *tenant in common* can reach only that tenant's share. The other cotenants retain their proportionate shares, which they can transfer to third parties. Partition also remains an option.

Example 9.17: G transferred land "to *A*, *B*, and *C* as tenants in common." *A* has accumulated substantial debts to *X*.

X may reach *A*'s share of the land, but not the shares of *B* and *C*.

The creditor of a *joint tenant* may (as with tenancy in common) seek partition. Short of partition, the creditor should act promptly to sever the estate, thereby transforming it into a tenancy in common. (This is typically done by the execution of a lien on the property then a judgment sale of the debtor-tenant's interest.) If the creditor fails to act while the debtor-tenant is alive, the creditor will be too late. The right of survivorship will operate at the debtor-tenant's death, leaving nothing within the creditor's reach.

Example 9.18: G transferred land "to *A*, *B*, and *C* as joint tenants and not as tenants in common." *A* has accumulated large debts to *X*.

X must act while *A* is alive to sever or partition the tenancy. If the land remains in joint tenancy the moment before *A*'s death, the right of survivorship leaves *B* and *C* as the owners, with nothing reachable by *X*.

The creditor of one spouse who holds property as a *tenant by the entirety* will generally be unable to reach the property. Most states recognizing the tenancy hold that it may be reached only by a creditor of both spouses. See *Sawada v. Endo*, 57 Haw. 608, 561 P.2d 1291 (1977). The U.S. Supreme Court recently held, however, that this rule of state law does not apply when the creditor is the federal government: in *United States v. Craft*, 535 U.S. 274 (2002), the Court upheld a federal tax lien imposed when one spouse, but not the other, owed substantial sums to the Internal Revenue Service.

Example 9.19: *G* transferred land "to *A* and *B*, husband and wife, as tenants by the entirety." *A* (but not *B*) has accumulated significant debts to *X*.

X cannot reach the land in most states recognizing the tenancy by the entirety, unless *X* is a branch of the federal government.

Before *Craft*, the tenancy by the entirety offered a protective shield to married persons by insulating the marital home from creditors. In the words of one case, "the archaic fiction of a tenancy by the entireties is preserved [in modern law] only because it makes it almost impossible for creditors to reach a debtor's family house." *Harris v. Crowder*, 174 W.Va. 83, 322 S.E.2d 854 (1984). The decision in *Craft* represents a noteworthy breach in this protective shield. Whether *Craft* will lead to the further erosion—perhaps even the complete abolition—of the tenancy by the entirety remains to be seen.

§ 9.7   Rights of the Surviving Spouse

The decedent's proportionate fraction of land held as *tenant in common* is devisable and descendible. Thus, if the decedent dies partially or completely intestate, the surviving spouse will receive an intestate share (see § 8.2). If the decedent's will devises the property to a third party, the surviving spouse will be entitled to an elective share (see § 8.3).

Land held by a decedent and a third party as *joint tenants* is neither devisable nor descendible. Rather, the right of survivorship automatically operates at the decedent's death. Nothing is left for the decedent's spouse to inherit or, under traditional law, to claim in the elective share. The Uniform Probate Code's elective share, however, takes the opposite approach. The UPC provides that the surviving spouse is entitled to an elective share in "[t]he decedent's fractional interest in property held by the decedent in joint tenancy ... to the extent the fractional interest passed by right of survivorship at the decedent's death to a surviving joint tenant other than the decedent's surviving spouse." UPC § 2-205(1)(ii).

> *Example 9.20:* G transferred land "to *A* and *B* as joint tenants and not as tenants in common." Later, *A* died, survived by his spouse, *S*.
>
> In many non-UPC jurisdictions, the land passes automatically at *A*'s death to *B* and cannot be reached by *S*'s elective share.
>
> Under the UPC, the land is subject to *S*'s elective share.

Property held by the decedent and the surviving spouse as *tenants by the entirety* passes automatically to the surviving spouse.

§ 9.8 A Footnote on Joint Bank Accounts

Joint bank and other financial organization accounts typically contain a survivorship feature. The balance on hand in the account at the death of a depositor shifts automatically to the surviving joint account holders without going through probate. Except in a very few states, however, the funds in a joint account are not owned in joint tenancy (or tenancy by the entirety, if between spouses). That is to say, a deposit into such an account does not in most states transfer an undivided interest therein to the other account holders. The fact that each account holder can as a matter of practice withdraw the whole of the account masks the true ownership of the funds. The true ownership is that each account holder owns only his or her contributions. See Uniform Probate Code § 6-211. If one co-account holder withdraws an amount in excess of his or her contributions, the other account holders normally have the right to force the excess to be returned.

EXERCISES ON PARTS II AND III

1. *G* transferred land "to *A*, *B*, and *C* as tenants in common." What happens if:

a. *A* transfers his interest to *X*?

b. *A* dies intestate, survived by his sole heir, *H*?

c. *A* dies, survived by his spouse, *S*, and with a will devising "all of my property to X-Charity"?

2. *G* transferred land "to *A*, *B*, and *C* as joint tenants and not as tenants in common." What happens if:

a. *A* transfers his interest to *X*?

b. *A* dies, survived by his sole heir, *H*?

c. *A* dies intestate, survived by his spouse, *S*, and with a will devising "all of my property to X-Charity"?

3. *G* transferred land "to *A*, *B*, and *C* as tenants in common with the right of survivorship." What result?

PART IV

POWERS OF APPOINTMENT

CHAPTER 10

A PRIMER ON POWERS

Professor W. Barton Leach described the power of appointment as "the most efficient dispositive device that the ingenuity of Anglo-American lawyers has ever worked out." Powers of Appointment, 24 A.B.A. J. 807 (1938). This device is the subject of the remaining chapters.

§ 10.1   Definitions and Terminology

A *power of appointment* is generally defined as the authority to designate recipients of beneficial interests in or powers of appointment over property. An owner, of course, has this authority with respect to his or her property. By creating a power of appointment, the owner confers this authority on someone who is not the property's owner.

The property subject to a power of appointment is called the *appointive property*. The property interest subject to appointment need not be an absolute-ownership interest. In fact, powers of appointment frequently involve appointment of a remainder interest, as in the following example.

> *Example 10.1:* G transferred property in trust, providing for "income to *A* for life, remainder in corpus to those of *A*'s descendants as *A* shall by will appoint; in default of appointment, to X-Charity."
>
> *A* subsequently died, leaving a will that exercised her power of appointment in favor of her adult child, *B*.

The parties connected to a power of appointment are identified by a special terminology. The *donor* is the person who created the power of appointment—*G* in the above example. The *donee* (powerholder) is the person upon whom the power of appointment was conferred—*A* in the above example.

The *objects* (permissible appointees) are the persons in whose favor the power can be exercised—*A*'s descendants in the above example.

The donor determines who the objects are by expressly designating them in the instrument creating the power. If the donor does not expressly designate objects, the donee is free in almost all states to appoint in favor of anyone in the world, including the donee, the donee's estate, the creditors of the donee, or the creditors of the donee's estate.

The *appointee* is the person to whom an appointment has been made—*B* in the above example. The appointment makes the appointee the owner of the appointed property interest.

The *taker in default* is the person who takes the appointive property to the extent that the power is not effectively exercised—X-Charity in the above example. The taker in default has a property interest that is subject to the power of appointment. Upon *A*'s death, X-Charity's property interest was divested in favor of the appointee, *B*.

In all cases, there is a donor, a donee, and someone in whose favor an appointment can be made. The other parties are not indispensable. The donee is under no duty to exercise a power of appointment and, therefore, appointees might not always exist. Also, the donor need not expressly designate takers in default.

§ 10.2 Powers are Personal

Powers of appointment are personal to the donee. If the donee dies without having exercised the power, the power expires. It cannot be passed to the donee's successors in interest.

§ 10.3 Classification of Powers

Powers of appointment are differentiated in many ways. Two of the most important distinctions are between presently exercisable and testamentary powers, and between general and nongeneral powers. Both of these distinctions relate to the scope of the donee's authority. An extremely important, overarching principle—followed in almost all states—is that the scope of the donee's authority is presumptively unlimited. That is, the donee's authority as to appointees and the time and manner of appointment is limited only to the extent the donor effectively manifests an intent to impose limits.

When the donee can exercise a power only in the donee's will, the power is called *testamentary*. When the donee can exercise the power either in an inter vivos instrument or in the donee's will, the power is called *presently exercisable*. (Sometimes the donee can exercise a power only in an inter vivos instrument. This type of power is sometimes described as a power exercisable by deed alone, although technically the power can be exercised by any instrument or act that is formally sufficient under applicable law to accomplish an inter vivos transfer.) Testamentary exercises of powers to appoint a remainder are rarely prohibited, but some powers, such as powers to revoke or amend a trust, or to invade the corpus of a trust, are generally thought to be inherently restricted to inter vivos exercises.

A *general* power is one that is exercisable in favor of the donee, the donee's estate, the donee's creditors, or the creditors of the donee's estate. A *nongeneral* power is one in which the donee, the donee's estate, the donee's creditors, and the creditors of the donee's estate are excluded as objects.

In accordance with the overarching presumption of unlimited authority, powers are assumed in most jurisdictions to be *general* and *presently exercisable* in the absence of express language indicating otherwise. An exception is Maryland, which requires express language in order to appoint to the donee, the donee's estate, or the creditors of either. See *Frank v. Frank*, 253 Md. 413, 253 A.2d 377 (1969).

The classifications are illustrated in the following examples.

Example 10.2: G transferred land "to A for life, remainder to such person or persons as A shall appoint; in default of appointment, remainder to B."

A holds a presently exercisable general power. It is presently exercisable because G did not expressly restrict the exercise of the power either to a will or to an inter vivos instrument. The power is general because G did not forbid A from exercising the power in A's own favor.

Example 10.3: G transferred land "to A for life, remainder to such of A's descendants as A shall by will appoint; in default of appointment, remainder to B."

A holds a nongeneral testamentary power. It is testamentary because G inserted the phrase "by will." Thus any purported inter vivos exercise of the power would be invalid. The power is nongeneral because *A* is authorized to appoint only among her own descendants, a group that doesn't include *A*. (The possibility that one of *A*'s descendants might turn out to be a creditor of *A* is ignored. See Restatement 2d of Property § 11.4 illus. 4.)

Another way that powers of appointment are differentiated is on the basis of the donee's property interest, if any, in the appointive property. There are three categories: collateral powers, powers in gross, and powers appendant.

A power is *collateral* if the donee owns no property interest in the appointive property.

A power is a *power in gross* if the donee has a property interest in the appointive property that cannot be affected by the exercise of the power. A power of appointment over the remainder interest held by the life tenant is a typical example.

A *power appendant* arises where the donee has a property interest in the appointive property that can be affected by the exercise of the power. In other words, the power of appointment purports to authorize the donee to divest the donee's own property interest and confer it on someone else. (As we shall see in the next section, powers appendant are invalid.)

The following examples illustrate the categories.

Example 10.4: G transferred land "to *A* for life, remainder to such person or persons as *P* shall appoint; in default of appointment, remainder to *B*."

P holds a collateral power. *P* has no interest in the appointive property other than the power of appointment itself.

Example 10.5: G transferred land "to *A* for life, remainder to such person or persons as *A* shall by will appoint; in default of appointment, remainder to *B*."

A holds a power in gross. *A* has an interest in the property (a life estate) but the life estate cannot be affected by *A*'s testamentary power.

Example 10.6: G transferred property in trust, providing for "income to *A* for life, then remainder in corpus to *B*." *A* is empowered by the trust instrument to direct the trustee to terminate the trust and pay the property outright to any one or more of *A*'s descendants as *A* by deed or will directs. (Observe that an exercise of the power during A's lifetime would cause the appointee to receive both B's remainder and A's remaining income interest. An exercise of the power in A's will would cause the appointee to receive only B's remainder, as A's income interest expires at A's death.)

A has a power appendant over the income interest in the trust and a power in gross over the remainder. As we shall see in the next section, the power appendant is invalid. Put differently: A is held to have no power of appointment over A's own income interest. Any transfer of the income interest occurs by A's action as its owner, not as the donee of a power.

§ 10.4   Invalid Powers

Powers of appointment are invalid if (1) they are powers appendant; (2) they have no ascertainable object; or (3) they violate the Rule Against Perpetuities.

Powers appendant are invalid because the power merges into the property interest owned by the donee and ceases to have any separate existence. This is readily illustrated with reference to the facts in Example 10.6. Suppose that during *A*'s lifetime, *A* instructs the trustee to terminate the trust and pay the property outright to *A*'s oldest child, *X*. By this action, *X* receives both *A*'s remaining income interest and *B*'s remainder interest in the corpus. In what capacity has *A* acted? With respect to *B*'s interest, which *A* never owned, *A* acted as the donee of a nongeneral power of appointment. With respect to *A*'s income interest, *A* acted as its owner, not as a power holder. The distinction has important federal gift tax consequences for *A*. The exercise of the nongeneral power over the remainder is nontaxable, see IRC § 2514; but the transfer of the income interest is a taxable gift.

A power of appointment is also invalid if it has *no ascertainable object*, meaning that the objects are described in a way that makes it impossible to identify any person who fits the donor's description of the objects. So long as the donee can appoint to at least one person who fits the donor's description, the courts uphold the power.

Example 10.7: *G* transferred land "to *A* for life, remainder to such of *A*'s friends as *A* may designate by his will, and in default of such designation, to X-Charity."

The objects of the power—*A*'s "friends"—are sufficiently identifiable by the donee (*A*) that a valid appointment to one or more of them may be made. See Restatement 2d of Property § 12.1 illus. 18.

Powers of appointment (other than presently exercisable general powers) are subject to the Rule Against Perpetuities. A power that *violates the Rule* is invalid and cannot be validly exercised. The question of whether a power is invalid under the Rule is discussed in Chapter 14.

§ 10.5   Creating a Power: The Problem of Ambiguous Language

A donor creates a power of appointment "if the transferor manifests an intent that [the transfer] shall do so and if the transfer is otherwise effective." Restatement 2d of Property § 12.1. The intent can be manifested by the donor either expressly or by implication. No particular language is necessary; the words "power of appointment" or "appoint" need not be used.

Example 10.8: G transferred property "to *A* for life, remainder, if *A* dies intestate, to *B*."

This might be construed as implying a general power in *A* to appoint by will. See Simes & Smith on Future Interests § 892.

Different courts have construed recurring ambiguous dispositive patterns differently and have reached results that are difficult to reconcile. When, for example, property is devised to a devisee "to be disposed of in [the devisee's] discretion," or words of similar import, a court might adopt one of three interpretations. One is that the devisee takes an absolute-ownership interest on the theory that the added language is without legal effect. A second interpretation views the language as negating ownership and creating only a power of appointment. A third interpretation, appearing in the case law where the devisee is a fiduciary (e.g., the decedent's executor), is that the language creates a mandatory power requiring the fiduciary to distribute the property, with the power held invalid if the class of objects is not sufficiently definite for the fiduciary to perform this task.

Another recurring and perplexing dispositive pattern is the devise to someone for life, remainder to the life tenant's "executors and administrators" or "estate" or some similar phrase. Courts have had great difficulty in deciding the import of this type of devise. Some courts hold that the life tenant takes a general power of appointment. Other courts hold that the life tenant takes a remainder interest. If the remainder to the life tenant's "executors and administrators" is conditioned on some event, such as "income to *A* for life, and if *A* dies with issue, to *A*'s executors and administrators," other possible interpretations arise. One possibility is that the language created a remainder interest in *A*'s issue. Another possibility is that *A* took a nongeneral power. Still another possibility is that *A* received a remainder in fee (in addition to the life estate) on condition that *A* leaves issue.

From the drafting perspective, these ambiguities should be avoided. Powers of appointment should be created using clear and express language.

CHAPTER 11

WHO OWNS THE APPOINTIVE PROPERTY?

§ 11.1 Donors and "Relation Back"

As a technical matter, there is no doubt that the donee of a power of appointment is not the owner of the appointive property. The conventional distinction between beneficial ownership and a power of appointment is stated in Restatement 2d of Property § 11.1 cmt. b:

The beneficial owner of an interest in property ordinarily has the power to transfer to others beneficial rights in the owned interest. This power is an incident of the owned interest and the transfer is directly from the owner to the beneficiary of the transfer. A power, however, is the authority to designate beneficial interests in property other than as an incident of the beneficial ownership of the property. When the power is exercised, it is the completion of the terms of a transfer that started with the creator of the power.

Upon the exercise of a power of appointment, the notion is that the appointed property passes directly from the donor to the appointee. This is called the *doctrine of "relation back"*: the donee's appointment is deemed to relate back to and become part of the *donor's* original instrument. The donee is viewed as the donor's agent, as it were; an appointment retroactively fills in the blanks in the original instrument.

> *Example 11.1: G* transferred property in trust, providing for "income to *A* for life, remainder to such of *A*'s descendants as *A* shall appoint." *A* makes an inter vivos appointment to his child, *C*.
>
> Under the doctrine of relation back, *A*'s appointment is viewed as changing *G*'s original disposition to read: "income to *A* for life, remainder to *C*."

Technical ownership aside, when it comes to the rights of the donee's creditors or surviving spouse, the law does not always follow the relation-back doctrine.[1] The likelihood that the donee will be treated as if he or she owned the appointive property is greater in the case of a reserved power—where the donor of the power is also the donee of the power—as distinguished from a power conferred on the donee by another. We consider these issues in the remaining sections of this chapter.

§ 11.2   Rights of the Donee's Creditors

The rights of the donee's creditors depend on whether the power was reserved or whether it was created in the donee by another.

If a *reserved* power of appointment was created in a transfer deemed to be in fraud of creditors, the

[1]This statement is also true with respect to federal taxation. The application of federal tax laws to the various kinds of powers of appointment is complicated and beyond the scope of this *Nutshell*. The following is offered as a general summary. Federal tax laws treat the donor-donee of a reserved power as still owning the appointive property, irrespective of whether the reserved power is general or nongeneral. If the power is not reserved but conferred upon the donee by another, federal tax laws treat the donee as the owner of the appointive property if the power is general. The donee of a nongeneral nonreserved power is not treated as the owner of the appointive property.

appointive assets can be subjected to the donor-donee's debts. A transfer is in fraud of creditors, according to § 4(a) of the Uniform Fraudulent Transfers Act, if the transfer was made (1) "with actual intent to hinder, delay, or defraud" or (2) "without receiving a reasonably equivalent value in exchange for the transfer" and the transferor "(i) was engaged or was about to engage in a business or a transaction for which the remaining assets of the [transferor] were unreasonably small in relation to the business or transaction; or (ii) intended to incur, or believed or reasonably should have believed that he would incur, debts beyond his ability to pay as they became due."

Even if the transfer was not in fraud of creditors, the appointive assets are subject to the claims of the donor-donee's creditors if the reserved power is general. It makes no difference whether the debt was incurred before or after the transfer creating the power.

Example 11.2: G transferred land "to *A* for life, remainder to such persons as *G* shall appoint, and in default of appointment, to *B*." *G* has incurred substantial debts.

G's creditors can reach the remainder.

Until recent years, an anomaly existed with respect to a reserved power to revoke, such as that contained in a revocable inter vivos trust. The Restatement of Property excluded powers to revoke from the definition of the term "power of appointment," making inapplicable the rule that a reserved power of appointment subjects the appointive assets to the claims of the donor-donee's creditors. See Restatement of Property § 318(2) and cmt. i. In line with this view, courts and authorities held that trust assets of a revocable trust were exempt from the claims of the settlor's creditors. Restatement 2d of Trusts § 330 cmt. o. Recent statutes and cases, however, have adopted the opposite rule: revocable trusts can be reached by the settlor's creditors. See *State Street Bank & Trust Co. v. Reiser*, 7 Mass.App.Ct. 633, 389 N.E.2d 768 (1979). This new understanding has been adopted by the Restatement 2d of Property, which specifically includes powers to revoke in the definition of a power of appointment. Restatement 2d of Property § 11.1 cmt. c. Under modern law, therefore, the creditors of the settlor of a revocable trust are entitled to have their claims satisfied out of trust assets. On this point, see Restatement 2d of Property §§ 13.3, 34.3; Restatement 3d of Trusts § 25 cmt. e; Uniform Trust Code § 505(a)(1).

Example 11.3: G transferred property to T, as trustee of G's revocable inter vivos trust, to pay "income to A for life, and at A's death to deliver the trust assets to B." G has incurred substantial debts.

Under modern law, G's creditors can reach the property in the trust.

With respect to powers *created in the donee by another*, the majority view at common law is that the donee is treated as the beneficial owner of the appointive property only if the power is general *and* if the donee exercises the power, either inter vivos or by will.[2] In a minority of jurisdictions, however, the donee is not treated as the owner, even if the power is general and exercised. (Of course, if the donee exercises the power in favor of

---

[2] In most jurisdictions this rule applies only to the extent that the donee's exercise was an effective exercise. A few states, however, follow the view that an ineffective exercise entitles the donee's creditors to reach the appointive assets. Note that even in the states adhering to the prevailing view, there are circumstances in which an ineffective exercise has the effect under state property law of including the appointive assets in the donee's probate estate (see § 13.6), at which point the assets become the donee's for all purposes, including creditors' rights.

himself or his estate, the appointed property becomes owned by him and creditors can reach it.) If the power is nongeneral, the donee's creditors cannot reach the appointive assets irrespective of whether the power is exercised.

Example 11.4: G transferred land "to *A* for life, remainder to such persons as *X* shall appoint, and in default of appointment, to *B*." *X* has incurred substantial debts.

Under the majority view, *X*'s creditors can reach the remainder only if *X* exercises the power. Under the minority view, *X*'s creditors cannot reach the remainder; whether or not *X* exercises the power is irrelevant.

Example 11.5: G transferred land "to *A* for life, remainder to such charities as *X* shall appoint, and in default of appointment, to *B*." *X* has incurred substantial debts.

X's creditors cannot reach the remainder, because the power is nongeneral.

A minority of states has enacted legislation that affects the rights of creditors of a donee of a power created in him by another. The laws are not uniform; some expand the rights of the donee's creditors, others restrict them. It is important to be aware of any such statute in your state.

A final word may be offered on the federal bankruptcy code, which implies that general powers pass to the donee's trustee in bankruptcy; nongeneral powers clearly do not. See 11 U.S.C. § 541(b)(1).

§ 11.3   Rights   of   the   Donee's Surviving Spouse

The elective-share rights of the donee's surviving spouse depend on whether the power of appointment was reserved or whether it was created in the donee by another.

We begin with *reserved* powers. The traditional rule (noted in § 8.3) is that the surviving spouse's elective share applies only to the decedent's probate estate. This typically excludes property subject to a power to revoke or to a reserved power of appointment. A few cases have held that the decedent's attempt during lifetime to transfer property into a revocable trust was a fraudulent or illusory transfer, hence void, rendering the property subject to the elective share—but these cases are not numerous.

Example 11.6: G transferred almost all of his assets into a revocable trust of which he was not a beneficiary. The beneficiaries were G's mistress, M, for her life, then a remainder in M's then-living descendants. Later G died, survived by M and by G's spouse, S.

Under the traditional law, S has no right to an elective share in the trust assets, unless a court would be willing to take the rare step of declaring G's transfer fraudulent or illusory.

Nonprobate assets are typically subject to the elective share only to the extent provided by statute. One such statute is the Uniform Probate Code. UPC § 2-205(1)(i) makes the elective share applicable to "property over which the decedent alone, immediately before death, held a presently exercisable general power of appointment" regardless of when or by whom the power was created. The definition of such a power includes "a power to revoke or invade the principal of a trust or other property arrangement." UPC § 2-201(6).

Example 11.7: Same facts as the previous example, except that the applicable law is the Uniform Probate Code.

The trust assets are fully subject to S's elective-share rights.

In addition, UPC § 2-205(2)(ii) makes the elective share applicable to property subject to a general power "exercisable by the decedent alone or in conjunction with any other person, or exercisable by a nonadverse party," but only if the power was created by the decedent during the decedent's marriage to the surviving spouse.

Example 11.8: G transferred almost all of his assets into an irrevocable inter vivos trust of which he was not a beneficiary. The beneficiaries were his mistress, M, for her life, then a remainder in such persons as G may by will appoint, and in default of appointment to M's then-living descendants. Later G died, survived by M and by G's spouse, S.

The Uniform Probate Code provides that the trust assets will be subject to S's elective-share rights, but only if the power was created during their marriage.

With respect to powers *created by the donee in another*, the traditional rule is that the surviving spouse cannot reach the appointive property against the wishes of the donee. This is true whether the power is general or nongeneral, presently exercisable or testamentary, exercised or unexercised. The explanation offered is that the surviving spouse's elective-share claim is against the donee's probate estate, and the appointive assets are not owned beneficially by the donee. The current version of the Uniform Probate Code, promulgated in 1990, broke new ground by including in the augmented estate "property over which the decedent alone, immediately before death, held a presently exercisable general power of appointment" regardless of when or by whom the power was created. UPC § 2-205(1)(i).

Example 11.9: G transferred land "to *A* for life, remainder to such persons as *X* shall appoint, and in default of appointment, to *B*." *X* then died, survived by his spouse, *S*.

Under traditional law, the land is not subject to *S*'s elective share. The Uniform Probate Code reaches the opposite result, on the ground that *X*'s presently exercisable general power gave *X* ownership of the land in substance if not in form.

CHAPTER 12

EXERCISING A POWER

§ 12.1   Capacity of the Donee

An effective appointment can only be made by a donee who has the requisite capacity. The capacity to make an effective appointment is the same capacity needed to make an effective transfer of the property if it were owned by the donee.

The capacity to make inter vivos and testamentary transfers is described in the Restatement 3d of Property § 8.1:

> If the donative transfer is in the form of a will, a revocable will substitute, or a revocable gift, the testator or donor must be capable of knowing and understanding in a general way the nature and extent of his or her property, the natural objects of his or her bounty, and the disposition that he or she is making of that

property, and must also be capable of relating these elements to one another and forming an orderly desire regarding the disposition of the property.

If the donative transfer is in the form of an irrevocable gift, the donor must have the mental capacity necessary to make or revoke a will and must also be capable of understanding the effect that the gift may have on the future financial security of the donor and of anyone who may be dependent on the donor.

Consider how these standards would apply to the following example.

Example 12.1: G transferred land "to *A* for life, then to such persons as *A* shall by will appoint, and in default of appointment, to *B*." *A*, believing that there were people living in the trees on the land, signed a will exercising the power of appointment in their favor so that they could be fed. No such tree-people existed.

A lacks the legal capacity to exercise the power of appointment by will. The attempted exercise is invalid, so the land passes at *A*'s death to *B* in fee simple absolute.

§ 12.2   Compliance With Formalities

An appointment must satisfy the formal conveyancing requirements that would be applicable to a transfer of the property if it were owned by the donee. A testamentary appointment, for example, must be contained in a validly executed will.

> *Example 12.2:* G transferred land "to A for life, then to such persons as X shall appoint, and in default of appointment, to B." Later X orally proclaimed that the property should pass at A's death to A's daughter, D.
>
> The attempted exercise of the power of appointment is ineffective. Statutes require the conveyance or devise of land to be in writing.

§ 12.3   Intent to Exercise

A donee must intend to exercise a power in order for the power to be exercised. The recommended method for exercising a power of appointment is by a direct-exercise clause:

> I hereby exercise the power of appointment conferred upon me by my mother's will of

[date] as follows: I appoint [fill in details of appointment].

Unfortunately, the recommended method is not always used. Often, a so-called blanket-exercise clause is used. A blanket-exercise clause purports to exercise "any power of appointment" the donee may have. Blanket-exercise clauses are typically found in blending clauses, which blend the appointive property with the donee's own property:

All the residue of my estate, including any property over which I have a power of appointment, I give as follows: [fill in details of devise].

(Note that a blending clause need not be a blanket-exercise clause. A clause providing "All the residue of my estate, including the property over which I have a power of appointment under my mother's will, I give as follows" is a blending clause but not a blanket-exercise clause.)

Blanket-exercise clauses express the donee's intent to exercise a power of appointment. They are not recommended, however, because they can raise a question about whether the exercise of the power complies with the formality of a specific reference commonly imposed by donors (see § 12.4) and because they may subject the appointive property to the claims of the donee's creditors (see § 11.2).

In the absence of an express exercise of a power, an intent by the donee to exercise the power can be implied. In the leading case of *Blagge v. Miles*, 1 Story 426, 3 F. Cas. 559 (C.C. Mass. 1841), the court described circumstances giving rise to an implied exercise:

> Three classes of cases have been held to be sufficient demonstrations of an intended execution of a power: (1) Where there has been some reference in the will, or other instrument, to the power; (2) or a reference to the property, which is the subject, on which it is to be executed; (3) or, where the provision in the will or other instrument, executed by the donee of the power, would otherwise be ineffectual, or a mere nullity; in other words, it would have no operation, except as an execution of the power.

The majority view at common law is that a residuary clause or other clause referring generally to "my estate" or "my property" does not exercise a power of appointment unless other facts establish intent.

A minority of jurisdictions, however, follows the so-called Massachusetts view, that rebuttably presumes that a residuary clause was intended to exercise a general power even though the clause makes no reference to powers. Massachusetts itself abrogated that view by adopting a statute similar to the pre-1990 version of UPC § 2-610, which codified the majority common-law view. See Mass. Gen. Laws ch. 191 § 1(A)(4).

The current version of the Uniform Probate Code adopts a variation of the minority view. Under UPC § 2-608, a general power is presumed exercised by a residuary clause, but only if the donor failed to create a gift in default of appointment. The aim is to avoid the appointive property returning to the donor's estate, which would need to be reopened if, as is likely, the donor predeceased the donee.

Example 12.3: G devised land "to A for life, then to such persons as A shall by will appoint." A later died with a will providing for the disposition of "all my property to C."

Under the majority view at common law, *A* has not exercised the power of appointment. At *A*'s death, the property reverts to *G* (i.e., *G*'s successors in interest).

Under the minority view and the UPC, *A* has exercised the power of appointment. It is not necessary to reopen *G*'s estate to identify his successors in interest. Instead, the land passes at *A*'s death to *C* in fee simple absolute.

§ 12.4   Specific-Reference Requirements

In creating powers of appointment, it has become common practice for donors to provide that the power can only be exercised by language that specifically refers to the power. Specific-reference requirements came into use to prevent the adverse tax consequences that would arise from the inadvertent exercise of pre-1942 powers. They are still in common use today even though the tax treatment of post-1942 powers is different.[1]

[1] For general powers created in the donee by another on or before October 21, 1942, the value of the appointive property is taxed in the donee's estate only if the power is exercised. For such powers created after that date, the value of the appointive property is taxed in the donee's estate regardless of whether the power is exercised. See IRC § 2041.

A frequently litigated question is whether a particular donee has made a sufficiently specific reference. The question typically arises when the donee has used a blanket-exercise clause—a clause referring simply to "any property over which I have a power of appointment."

There is a split of authority on this question. Some judicial decisions and the Restatement 2d of Property § 17.1 illus. 1 state that a blanket-exercise clause does not satisfy a specific-reference requirement. See *First Nat'l Bank v. Walker*, 607 S.W.2d 469 (Tenn. 1980). Other decisions and § 2-704 of the Uniform Probate Code take the opposite view, that a blanket-exercise clause can satisfy a specific-reference requirement, especially where there is evidence that the donee knew of and intended to exercise the power and where there is no evidence that the donor intended to be so restrictive as to prevent any exercise not referring specifically to the power or the creating instrument. See *Motes/Henes Trust v. Motes*, 297 Ark. 380, 761 S.W.2d 938 (1988). Consider the following example.

Example 12.4: G devised property in trust "to T, to pay the income to A for life, then to deliver the trust property to such persons as A shall by will appoint, specifically referring to this power of appointment, and in default of exercise, to B." Later A executed a will, intending to exercise the power. The will's residuary clause gives "all of my property, including any property over which I may have a power of appointment, to X."

Under the approach of the Restatement 2d of Property, A has not effectively exercised the power of appointment; the property instead passes at A's death to B in fee simple absolute. UPC § 2-704 reaches the opposite result: the exercise is effective because there is evidence that A intended to exercise the power and no evidence that G intended to prevent an exercise in this fashion.

We prefer the UPC's flexible presumptions over the Restatement 2d's bright-line rule.

CHAPTER 13

EFFECTIVENESS OF THE APPOINTMENT

§ 13.1   Deceased Appointees

An exercise of a power of appointment in favor of a deceased person is ineffective, except as saved by an antilapse statute. (For students who have not yet covered this material in Trusts and Estates: antilapse statutes typically provide that if a devisee fails to survive the testator, a substitute gift is created in the devisee's descendants who survive the testator. The statutes usually apply only to devisees who are relatives or specified relatives of the testator.)

Antilapse statutes in states that have not adopted the Uniform Probate Code are commonly silent as to whether they apply to the exercise of a power of appointment. Nevertheless, these statutes usually are held to apply to the testamentary exercise of a general power in favor of a deceased appointee, as long as the appointee is in the protected relationship to—a relative, or a specified relative, of—the donee of the power. As to a nongeneral power, the authority that exists suggests that the statute applies only if the appointee is in the protected relationship *and* the substituted takers specified in the antilapse statute are objects of the power.

The UPC's antilapse statute expressly applies to the exercise of a power of appointment, by defining "devisee" as including "an appointee under a power of appointment exercised by the testator's will" if the appointee is a "grandparent, a descendant of a grandparent or a stepchild of either the testator or the donor of the power." UPC § 2-603(a)(4), (b).

Consider the following example.

Example 13.1: (1) G devised land "to *A* for life, remainder to such persons as *A* shall by will appoint, and in default of appointment, to *B*."

(2) G devised land "to *A* for life, remainder to such of *A*'s descendants as *A* shall by will appoint, and in default of appointment, to *B*."

A executed a will exercising her power of appointment in favor of her son, *S*. *S* predeceased *A*, leaving three of *S*'s children who survived *A*.

In both Variations, an antilapse statute would create a substitute appointment in S's children who survived *A*.

UPC § 2-603 and the Restatement 3d of Property § 5.5 cmt. l provide that the substitute gift is not defeated merely because the substitute takers are not objects of the power. UPC § 2-603(b)(5) states that "a surviving descendant of a deceased appointee of a power of appointment can be substituted for the appointee ... whether or not the descendant is an object of the power."

Example 13.2: Same facts as Variation (2) above, except that the objects of the power are not *A*'s "descendants" but *A*'s "children."

Under the UPC and Restatement 3d, the substitute appointment in *S*'s children (*A*'s grandchildren) is still created, even though the nongeneral power was limited to *A*'s children.

§ 13.2 The Creation of Interests Short of Absolute Ownership

A question that sometimes arises is whether the donee of a power of appointment must appoint the property absolutely (if land, in fee simple absolute) or whether the donee can create limited or future interests in the appointees. The answer is that, absent the donor's manifested contrary intention, the donee may do so. Furthermore, if the power is a general power, the donee may create limited interests even where the donor has explicitly prohibited it, because attempting to enforce the prohibition would be useless; the donee could simply appoint to himself outright and then transfer the property in a more limited fashion.

Example 13.3: G transferred land "to *A* for life, remainder to such persons as *A* shall appoint, and in default of appointment, to *B*." *A* exercised the power to create a life estate in his son, *S*, followed by a remainder in *S*'s descendants who survive *S*.

A has validly exercised the power. Because the power is general, this exercise would be valid even if *G* had expressly restricted the exercise to transfers in fee simple absolute.

§ 13.3   The Creation of a New Power

The donee of a general power can confer a power of appointment, general or nongeneral, on the appointee.

With respect to a nongeneral power, the better view is that the donee can create a general power in the appointee. After all, the donee could have appointed outright to the appointee, and conferring a general power is the equivalent. A few courts have held to the contrary; these courts object to the ability of the second donee to exercise his power in favor of nonobjects of the original power.

The donee of a nongeneral power can create a nongeneral power in an appointee, as long as the objects of the second power do not include anyone who is not an object of the first. This limitation may seem odd, but it is explained by the theory that the original donee is, in effect, delegating to the second donee the final selection of appointees. Restatement 2d of Property § 19.4 cmt. a.

Example 13.4: G transferred land "to A for life, remainder to such of A's descendants as A shall by will appoint, and in default of appointment, to B."

(1) *A*'s will exercised the power of appointment by devising the land "to such persons as my son, *S*, shall appoint."

(2) *A*'s will exercised the power of appointment by devising the land "to such charities as my son, *S*, shall appoint."

According to the Restatement 2d, *A*'s exercise is valid in Variation (1) but not in Variation (2). The latter result occurs because the objects of *S*'s nongeneral power are not objects of *A*'s nongeneral power.

§ 13.4   Appointments to Nonobjects

The exercise of a nongeneral power in favor of a person who is not an object is ineffective. This is true whether the appointment is made directly to the nonobject or whether it is made indirectly (to an object for the purpose of benefitting the nonobject). Such an indirect appointment is called a *fraud on the power*.

Example 13.5: *G* transferred land "to *A* for life, remainder to such of *A*'s descendants as *A* shall appoint, and in default of appointment to *B*." *A*'s exercise favored her husband, *H*.

A's exercise is ineffective. At *A*'s death, the land passes to *B* in fee simple absolute.

§ 13.5   Appointments to Takers in Default

There is disagreement among the cases as to the effectiveness of an appointment to a taker in default. Some cases hold that such an appointment is ineffective, because the taker in default holds an interest created by the donor that can be defeated or changed by the exercise of the power, but an exercise in conformity with the taker's interest is a mere nullity.

The capacity in which the person takes, as appointee or as taker in default, is of no great concern to the person taking. The significance of whether the appointment is effective lies elsewhere. The question usually arises in cases of general powers and the claims of the donee's creditors, usually creditors of the donee's estate. By the majority common-law view, an ineffective appointment of a general power does not allow creditors to reach the appointive assets. (Recall the discussion in § 11.2.)

Example 13.6: G transferred land "to *A* for life, remainder to such persons, including *X*'s estate, as *X* shall by will appoint, and in default of appointment, to *B*." *X* died having accumulated substantial debts. He exercised the power of appointment in his will, devising the land to *B*.

Whether the exercise is deemed effective depends upon the jurisdiction. If the exercise is deemed ineffective, the majority of jurisdictions would then hold that the creditors of *X*'s estate may not reach the land.

§ 13.6   Failure to Exercise; Ineffective Exercise

If the donee of a power fails to exercise the power, the appointive assets pass to the takers in default. If there is no gift-in-default clause, what happens to the property depends on whether the power is general or nongeneral. If a general power is unexercised, the appointive assets revert to the donor (or the donor's successors in interest). If a nongeneral power is unexercised or if the appointment is ineffective, the appointive property will go to the objects of the power if the objects are a defined limited class. Two different theories are employed to reach the latter result. Some courts hold that the donee of a nongeneral power with a defined limited class of objects has the duty to exercise the power, i.e., that the power is a power in trust (also called an imperative or mandatory power), and the court will not permit the objects to suffer by the negligence of the donee. Other courts imply a gift in default in favor of the objects.

Example 13.7: The objects of *A*'s nongeneral power are *A*'s children; there is no express gift in default. *A* dies without exercising the power or makes an ineffective appointment.

The appointive assets will go to *A*'s children who survive *A* (and substituted takers for a deceased child, if an antilapse statute applies). Both the power-in-trust theory and the implied-gift-in-default theory lead to this result. If, however, there are no objects to whom the property can pass, the appointive assets revert to the donor (or the donor's successors in interest).

Example 13.8: The objects of *A*'s nongeneral power are anyone in the world except *A*, *A*'s estate, and the creditors of either. *A* dies without exercising the power or makes an ineffective appointment.

The appointive assets revert to the donor (or the donor's successors in interest). The power is not a power in trust and there is no implied gift in default, because the objects of the power are not a defined limited class.

There is a special rule governing the ineffective exercise (as opposed to failure to exercise) of a general power. The usual result is that the property goes to the takers in default or, if none, reverts to the donor (or the donor's successors in interest). If, however, the donee's appointment manifests an intent to assume control of the property for all purposes and not merely for the limited purpose of giving effect to the expressed appointment, courts apply the *capture doctrine*, which means that the appointive property goes to the donee's estate.

The donee's intent to assume control of the property is manifested (and the capture doctrine is triggered) by: (1) a blanket-exercise clause, described in § 12.3; (2) a residuary clause that presumptively demonstrates an intent to exercise the power, pursuant to a statute or rule of common law; (3) a residuary clause that demonstrates an intent to exercise the power because the donee's estate is insufficient to satisfy the donee's devises;

or (4) in the view of some but not all courts, an appointment in trust.

To protect against the capture doctrine, donors should introduce the gift-in-default clause with the phrase: "To the extent the donee does not expressly exercise this power of appointment effectively,..."

§ 13.7 Releases of Powers

The Restatement 2d of Property §§ 14.1 and 14.2 declare that all powers of appointment, general and nongeneral, testamentary and presently exercisable, are releasable in whole or in part, unless the donor has effectively manifested an intent that the power not be releasable.

If the donor of a general power expressly provides that the power cannot be released, the donor's intention may not be effective. The restriction must still be examined under the rules governing unreasonable restraints on alienation. Restatement 2d of Property § 14.1 cmt. a.

An express provision prohibiting the release of a nongeneral power is probably valid. Apart from an express prohibition, the release of a nongeneral power is impliedly prohibited if the nongeneral power is a power in trust (also called an imperative or mandatory power), i.e., where the objects are a defined limited class and the donor has not provided for a disposition of the property in case the power is not exercised.

The release of a power of appointment, when permissible, is effectively an exercise in favor of the takers in default, even where an actual exercise in favor of a taker in default would be ineffective (e.g., because a taker died prior to the release).

Example 13.9: *G*'s will devised property in trust, to pay the income to *A* for life, then to pay the trust corpus to such of *A*'s children as *A* shall by will appoint; in default of appointment, to *A*'s children equally. *G* was survived by *A* and *A*'s children, *X* and *Y*. *X* then died, leaving all his estate to his wife, *W*. Then *A* released her power of appointment.

The release made the gift in default in favor of *A*'s children indefeasibly vested. At *A*'s death, the corpus of the trust will go to *Y* and *X*'s successor in interest (*W*).

CHAPTER 14

POWERS AND THE RULE AGAINST PERPETUITIES

§ 14.1   The Rule and "Relation Back"

Recall the *doctrine of "relation back"* from Chapter 11: the donee's appointment is deemed to relate back to and become part of the donor's original instrument. As we saw in that chapter, the doctrine is sometimes followed, sometimes not.

When relation back is not followed, it is usually because the nature of the power puts the donee's relationship to the appointive property close enough in substance to that of an outright owner that, for the purposes of the particular question involved, the property should be treated as if owned by the donee.

The Rule Against Perpetuities follows or rejects

relation back on this basis. For perpetuity purposes, as we shall see, the relation back theory is generally followed for nongeneral powers and for general testamentary powers but rejected for presently exercisable general powers.

With the above background in mind, we can now consider how the common-law Rule and the Uniform Rule apply to powers of appointment. It is important to distinguish between the *validity of the power itself* and the *validity of the exercise of the power*. If a power of appointment itself violates the Rule Against Perpetuities, the power is invalid, and the disposition takes effect as if the power had never been created. If the power itself is valid, it may be exercised in such a way that creates contingent property interests; these interests created by its exercise may violate the Rule and be invalid.

§ 14.2   Presently Exercisable General Powers

Under the common-law Rule and the Uniform Rule, a general power that is presently exercisable is treated as the equivalent of a *vested* property interest *in the donee* (rejecting relation back). As a vested interest, the power itself is not subject to either Rule.

Example 14.1: G devised land "to A for life, remainder to such persons as A shall appoint, and in default of appointment, to B."

A's presently exercisable general power of appointment is treated as vested, hence not subject to the common-law Rule or to the Uniform Rule.

One must still determine the validity of the power's *exercise*. In determining this, the *donee* (not the donor) is considered to have created the appointed interests. Put differently: the exercise is treated as if the donee first exercised the power in his or her own favor and then created the appointed interests out of owned property. Consequently, the appointed interests are created, for purposes of the Rule, when the exercise of the power becomes effective. (On "time of creation" see § 5.7.)

The only change in the above analysis effected by the Uniform Rule is that an exercise that would have been invalid at common law is not initially invalid, but instead is subject to wait-and-see. The 90-year period applies in determining the validity of appointed interests that would have been invalid at common law.

Consider the following example.

Example 14.2: A was the income beneficiary of a trust and the donee of a presently exercisable general power over the succeeding remainder interest. *A* exercised the power by deed, directing the trustee after *A*'s death to pay the income to *A*'s children in equal shares for the life of the survivor, and upon the death of the last surviving child to pay the corpus of the trust to her then-living grandchildren.

Under the common-law Rule, the validity of the appointed interests depends on whether *A*'s appointment was irrevocable. If *A* reserved a power to revoke the appointment, the appointed interests are deemed created at *A*'s death and are valid. If *A*'s appointment was irrevocable, however, the interests were created when the deed was delivered or otherwise became effective, and the remainder interest in *A*'s grandchildren invalid.

Under the Uniform Rule, the outcome is the same, except that if *A*'s appointment was irrevocable, the remainder in *A*'s grandchildren is not initially invalid. Instead, it is valid if *A*'s last surviving child dies within 90 years after *A*'s death.

§ 14.3   General   Powers   Not Presently Exercisable Because of a Condition Precedent

If a general power would be presently exercisable but for the fact that its exercise is subject to a condition precedent, the power is treated by both the common-law Rule and the Uniform Rule as the equivalent of a *nonvested* property interest *in the donee* (rejecting relation back). Remember that a power of appointment expires on the donee's death (§ 10.2), and so a deferral of a power's exercisability until a future time—even a time certain—imposes a condition precedent, the condition precedent being that the donee must be alive at that future time.

Under the common-law Rule, a general power not presently exercisable because of a condition precedent is invalid unless the condition precedent must be resolved one way or the other within a life in being plus 21 years. Consequently, an unborn person can be the recipient of a valid general power that becomes presently exercisable upon the donee's birth. To be valid, of course, the donee's birth must be certain to occur, if it ever occurs, within a life in being plus 21 years.

Under the Uniform Rule, a general power not presently exercisable because of a condition precedent is initially valid if it satisfies the common-law Rule. If it does not satisfy the common-law Rule, however, the power is not automatically invalid. Instead, the power is valid if the condition precedent actually occurs within the 90-year period; if it does not, the disposition can be reformed to make it valid.

These principles are illustrated in the following example.

Example 14.3: G devised land "to *A* for life, then to *A*'s first born child for life, then to such persons as *A*'s first born child shall appoint." *G* was survived by *A*, who is childless.

Under the common-law Rule, the general power conferred upon *A*'s first born child is valid. The condition precedent—that *A* have a child—is certain to be resolved one way or the other within *A*'s lifetime; *A* is the validating life. If, however, the relevant language had been "then to such persons as *A*'s first born child shall appoint after reaching age 25," the age contingency would invalidate the general power at common law.

Under the Uniform Rule, the outcome is the same, except that if the power in A's first born child was contingent on reaching age 25, the power would not be initially invalid. Instead, it would be valid if A's first born child reaches age 25 within 90 years after A's death.

If a general power that was once not presently exercisable because of a condition precedent is valid and becomes presently exercisable, the validity of an exercise is governed by the same principles discussed in § 14.2.

§ 14.4   Nongeneral Powers and General Testamentary Powers

To be valid under the common-law Rule, a nongeneral power (whether testamentary or presently exercisable) or a general testamentary power cannot be *exercisable* beyond a life in being plus 21 years.[1] Underpinning this rule is the theory

---

[1] Discretionary powers held by fiduciaries (e.g., trustees) are nongeneral powers of appointment for perpetuity purposes. Discretionary fiduciary powers include a trustee's power to invade the corpus of a trust for the benefit of the income beneficiary, or a trustee's power to accumulate the income or pay it out among a group of beneficiaries. Under the

of relation back—the theory that any property interest created by the donee's exercise of a nongeneral power or of a general testamentary power is created by the donor *when the donor created the power*. Because no such property interest can vest until the power is exercised, the common-law Rule requires certainty that the power cannot be exercised beyond a life in being plus 21 years.

The Uniform Rule also follows the basic theory of relation back for nongeneral and general testamentary powers. Under the Uniform Rule, a nongeneral power or a general testamentary power that would be valid at common law is valid. The change effected by the Uniform Rule is that a nongeneral or a general testamentary power that would be invalid at common law is not initially invalid. Instead, the power is valid if it is actually exercised within 90 years after it was created.

Consider the following example.

---

common-law Rule, such powers are invalid if they might be exercised beyond a life in being plus 21 years. Under the Uniform Rule, powers that would have been invalid at common law can be exercised for 90 years.

Purely administrative fiduciary powers, such as the power to sell and reinvest trust assets, are not subject to either Rule.

Example 14.4: (1) G devised land "to *A* for life, then to *A*'s first born child for life, then to such persons as *A*'s first born child shall by will appoint;" or

(2) G devised land "to *A* for life, then to *A*'s first born child for life, then to such of *A*'s grandchildren as *A*'s first born child shall appoint."

G was survived by *A*, who is childless.

Under the common-law Rule, the power of appointment conferred upon *A*'s first born child—a general testamentary power in Variation (1), a nongeneral power presently exercisable in Variation (2)—is invalid. The latest possible time of exercise is at the death of *A*'s first born child, who cannot be the validating life because he or she was not "in being" at the creation of the power. The lesson under the common-law Rule is that a nongeneral or general testamentary power cannot validly be conferred on an unborn person, unless a perpetuity saving clause limits the power's exercisability to a life in being plus 21 years.

Under the Uniform Rule, the power in *A*'s first born child is not initially invalid. It is valid if *A*'s first born child exercises the power within 90 years after *G*'s death. Note that a testamentary exercise takes place when the donee dies, not when the donee signs his or her will. Thus, in Variation (1), *A*'s first born child must die within 90 years after G's death in order for the child's power to be valid. In Variation (2), the child must also die within 90 years after *G*'s death if the child chooses to exercise the power by will rather than by deed.

If a nongeneral or a general testamentary power is valid, it can be validly exercised. Whether or not the exercise *is* valid is the next question.

Both the common-law Rule and the Uniform Rule apply the theory of relation back in determining the validity of interests created by the exercise of these types of powers. Thus, any property interest created by the donee's exercise is treated as created by the donor *when the donor created the power.*

Once the time of creation is pinpointed, both the common-law Rule and the Uniform Rule basically apply the same rules to appointed interests as they apply to interests created by an owner of property. At common law, contingent interests must be certain to vest, if at all, within a life in being (at the creation of the power) plus 21 years. Under the Uniform Rule, contingent interests that do not satisfy the common-law Rule are valid if they vest within 90 years after the creation of the power.

Consider the following examples.

Example 14.5: (1) A was the life income beneficiary of a trust and the donee of a nongeneral power over the succeeding remainder interest.

(2) A was the life income beneficiary of a trust and the donee of a general testamentary power over the succeeding remainder interest

In both cases, the trust was created by the will of *A*'s mother, *G*, who predeceased him. *A* exercised his power by will, directing the income to be paid after his death to his brother *B*'s children for the life of the survivor of them, and upon the death of *B*'s last surviving child, to pay the corpus of the trust to *B*'s then-living grandchildren. *B* predeceased *G*; *B* was survived by his two children, *X* and *Y*, who also survived *G* and *A*.

Under both the common-law Rule and the Uniform Rule, *A*'s appointment in either Variation is valid. The remainder interest in *B*'s grandchildren was created at *G*'s death when the power was created, not on *A*'s death when the power was exercised. Since *B* was dead at *G*'s death, the validating lives are *X* and *Y*.

Example 14.6: Suppose that in the preceding example *A* exercised his power by will, directing the income to be paid after his death to his own children for the life of the survivor, and upon the death of *A*'s last surviving child, to pay the corpus of the trust to *A*'s then-living grandchildren. Suppose also that at *G*'s death, *A* had two children, *X* and *Y*, and that a third child *Z* was born later. *X*, *Y*, and *Z* all survived *A*.

Under the common-law Rule, the remainder interest in *A*'s grandchildren is treated as created by *G* when *G* died and is therefore invalid.

In Variation (1), where *A*'s power was a nongeneral power, at least one jurisdiction has non-uniform legislation providing that, for perpetuity purposes, the appointed interests were created when *A* exercised his power, not when his mother created his power. See Del. Code tit. 25 § 501. Under this view, the remainder interest in *A*'s grandchildren would be valid. *A*'s children would be the validating lives.

In Variation (2), where *A*'s power was a general testamentary power, a small number of jurisdictions have non-uniform legislation providing (and at least one common-law court has held) that, for perpetuity purposes, the appointed interests were created when *A* exercised his power, not when his mother created his power. See Del. Code tit. 25 § 501; S.D. Cod. Laws § 43-5-5; Wis. Stat. § 700.16; *Industrial Nat'l Bank v. Barrett*, 101 R.I. 89, 220 A.2d 517 (1966). Again under this view, the remainder interest in *A*'s grandchildren would be valid. *A*'s children would be the validating lives.

Under the Uniform Rule, the remainder interest in *A*'s grandchildren is treated as created when *G* died, not when *A* exercised his power. Unlike the rule at common law, however, the remainder interest is not initially invalid. It is valid if *A*'s last surviving child dies within 90 years after *G*'s death.

These examples illustrate that, for perpetuity purposes, interests created by the exercise of nongeneral powers or of general testamentary powers are generally treated as created when the power was created. It is also true that the facts existing when the power was exercised can be taken into account. Taking this "second look" at the facts is a well-established procedure. The *second-look doctrine* is illustrated in the following example.

Example 14.7: Same disposition and appointment as in Example 14.5. At *G*'s death, *A* had two children, *X* and *Y*, but, unlike Example 14.5, *A* had no additional children after *G*'s death, and at *A*'s death *X* and *Y* were still living.

Under the common-law Rule and the Uniform Rule, *A*'s appointment is valid. The remainder interest is created at *G*'s death.

If only the facts existing at that point could be taken into account, the remainder interest would be invalid under the common-law Rule and would be allowed 90 years after *G*'s death to vest under the Uniform Rule. Under the second-look doctrine, however, the facts existing at *A*'s death can be taken into account. Taking these facts into account saves *A*'s appointment. At *A*'s death, it has become clear that no additional children were born to *A* after

G's death. Thus A's last surviving child will be either X or Y, both of whom were "in being" at G's death and therefore constitute the validating lives.

Note that if, after A's death, a third child (Z) was born to A, this would make the remainder in A's grandchildren invalid if Z survived A (this was the situation in Example 14.5). If Z predeceased A, however, the grandchildren's remainder would be validated by the second-look doctrine.

The second-look doctrine is a departure from the fundamental principle under the common-law Rule Against Perpetuities that only the facts existing when the contingent property interest was *created* can be taken into account in determining validity (see § 5.7). A persuasive justification put forward for this departure is that until the appointment is made the appointed interests cannot be known and their validity cannot be litigated. Thus no useful purpose would be served by holding appointed interests to be invalid because of what might have happened after the power was created but which at the time of exercise can no longer happen.

Another way of understanding and perhaps

justifying the second-look doctrine is this. Restricting consideration to the facts existing when the power was created is out of the question. One post-creation fact that must be considered is the nature of the donee's appointment itself. If this fact could not be considered, no appointment, regardless of its terms, could ever be valid under the common-law Rule because of the *possibility* of the donee making an invalid appointment. Thus the nature of the actual appointment must be considered even though it is an event that occurred after the power was created. Although this amounts to taking a second look to determine the terms of the appointment, the process is rarely so described. Rather, if it is discussed at all, it is viewed as part of the fiction that the appointment "relates back" to the date of the power's creation. Some may therefore find it attractive to think of the second-look doctrine as nothing more than viewing the facts existing when the power was exercised as relating back along with the terms of the appointment.

A few cases and authorities have extended the second-look doctrine to gifts-in-default. See *Sears v. Coolidge*, 329 Mass. 340, 108 N.E.2d 563 (1952); *In re Frank*, 40 Pa. 116, 389 A.2d 536

(1978); Am. L. Prop. § 24.36; but see Simes & Smith on Future Interests § 1276. Under this approach, the gift-in-default clause is judged on the facts existing at the time of *non*-exercise. Consider the following example.

Example 14.8: *A* was the life income beneficiary of a trust and the donee of a nongeneral power over the succeeding remainder interest. In default of appointment, the income after *A*'s death was to be paid to his children for the life of the survivor, and on the death of *A*'s last surviving child, the corpus was to be paid to *A*'s then-living grandchildren. *A*'s mother, *G*, who predeceased him, created the trust in her will. At *G*'s death, *A* had two children, *X* and *Y*. *A* died without having additional children and without exercising the power. *A* was survived by *X* and *Y*.

The gift-in-default was created at *G*'s death. Nevertheless, a second look at the facts existing on *A*'s death validates the gift-in-default under both the common-law Rule and the Uniform Rule. The validating lives are *X* and *Y*. Without a second look, the remainder interest in *A*'s grandchildren would be invalid under the common-law Rule and subject to the 90-year permissible vesting period under the Uniform Rule. When *G* died, there was a possibility that *A* might have an additional child later, that such after-born child might survive *A*, and that such child might have a child (a grandchild of *A*) more than 21 years after the death of the survivor of *A*, *X*, and *Y*.

§ 14.5   Appointed Powers

The donee of a power of appointment might exercise it by creating another power of appointment. The validity of the appointed power and the validity of its exercise are governed by the principles set forth in the preceding sections. Consider the following example.

Example 14.9: *G* devised land to *A* for life, remainder to such of *A*'s descendants as *A* shall appoint. At his death, *A* exercised his nongeneral power by appointing to his child *B* for life, remainder to such of *B*'s descendants as *B* shall appoint. At her death, *B* exercised her nongeneral power by appointing to her child *C* for life, remainder to *C*'s children.

A and *B* were living at *G*'s death. *C* was born after *G*'s death. *A* died after *C* was born, survived by *B* and *C*. *B* then died survived by *C*.

B's power is valid under the common-law Rule and under the Uniform Rule. *B* is the validating life because *B* was alive at *G*'s death and cannot exercise her nongeneral power beyond her own death. If *B* had been born after *G*'s death, however, *B*'s power would have been invalid under the common-law Rule and would have been given 90 years after *G*'s death to be exercised under the Uniform Rule.

Although *B*'s power is valid, her exercise is partly invalid under the common-law Rule. The remainder in *C*'s children violates the Rule because it is subject to increase beyond a life in being at *G*'s death plus 21 years. Since *B*'s power was a nongeneral power, *B*'s appointment relates back and is treated as having been made by *A*. If *B*'s appointment related back no farther than that, of course, it would have been valid because *C* was alive at *A*'s death. However, *A*'s power was also a nongeneral power, so *B*'s appointment relates back another step. Because *B*'s appointment is now absorbed into *A*'s appointment, it is treated as having been made by *G*. Since *C* was not alive at *G*'s death, he cannot be the validating life. And, since *C* might have more children more than 21 years after the deaths of *A* and *B* and any other person who was "in being" at *G*'s death, the remainder in *C*'s children is invalid.

Under the Uniform Rule, the remainder in *C*'s children is not initially invalid. Instead, it is valid if *C* dies within 90 years after *G*'s death.

One might also consider the following variations on this example. If either *A*'s power or *B*'s power (or both) had been a general testamentary power rather than a nongeneral power, the above analysis would not change. However, if either *A*'s power or *B*'s power (or both) had been a general power presently exercisable, *B*'s appointment would have been valid under the common-law Rule and under the Uniform Rule. *C* would have been the validating life. (If *A* had the general power presently exercisable, the remainder in *C*'s children would be treated as having been created at *A*'s death, when *C* was alive; and if the general power presently exercisable were held by *B*, the remainder in *C*'s children would be treated as having been created at *B*'s death, when *C* was alive.)

EXERCISES ON PART IV

1. Identify the parties to, and classify, the following powers of appointment:

a. *G* transferred land "to *A* for life, remainder to such persons as *D* shall appoint, otherwise to *T*."

b. *G* transferred land "to *A* for life, remainder to such charities as *D* shall appoint, otherwise to *T*."

c. *G* transferred land "to *A* for life, remainder to such charities as *A* shall by will appoint, otherwise to *T*."

d. *G* transferred property in trust, "to pay the income to *A* for life, then to distribute the corpus to X-Charity. However, *A* may at any time direct the trustee to pay the trust corpus outright to *B*."

2. *G* conveyed property into a revocable trust providing for the payment of income to *A* for life, then for outright distribution of the corpus to such persons as *X* may appoint, otherwise to *B*. *G* died with substantial debts. *X* died without exercising the power, but with substantial debts and a surviving spouse, *S*. What result?

ANSWERS TO EXERCISES

Part I

1.a. *A* has a life estate. *G* has an indefeasibly vested reversion.

b. *A* has a term of years. *B* has an indefeasibly vested remainder. *G* retains nothing.

c. *A* has a term of years. *B* has a contingent remainder. *G* has a reversion that is vested subject to divestment.

d. *A* has a life estate. *B* and *C* have alternative contingent remainders. *G* has a technical reversion.

e. *A* has a life estate. *B* and *C* have contingent remainders (*C*'s remainder is subject to two contingencies). *G* has a reversion that is vested subject to divestment.

f. *A* has a life estate. *B* has a remainder that is vested subject to divestment. *C* has a shifting executory interest, which is contingent (based on the condition precedent that *B* not survive *A*). If *B* dies before *A*, *C*'s interest becomes an indefeasibly vested remainder.

311

2.a. *D* has a remainder that is vested subject to open. The unborn or unadopted children of *A* have executory interests contingent on being born or adopted and on reaching age 30. The class is open at *G*'s death to future children—in other words, the rule of convenience does not then apply—because the time of distribution is *A*'s death, not *G*'s death. The validity of the class gift is governed by the all-or-nothing rule. The executory interests are invalid, so the entire class gift is invalid.

b. The interest in the first child of *A* to reach age 30 is a contingent remainder. In a jurisdiction without the rule of the destructibility of contingent remainders, the interest is invalid under the Rule Against Perpetuities, because there is no validating life. (*D* might not be the first child to reach age 30.) In a jurisdiction with the destructibility rule, however, the interest is valid: the contingent remainder will either vest in possession or be destroyed at *A*'s death, so *A* is the validating life.

c. Before evaluating the effect of the Rule, one must classify the interests. *G* has created a term of years in *A*, followed by a remainder in *G*'s "heirs at law." This remainder triggers the doctrine of worthier title in the jurisdictions still recognizing the doctrine. In such jurisdictions, the remainder in

G's heirs becomes a reversion in *G*. Reversions are always vested, hence not subject to the Rule Against Perpetuities. In a jurisdiction not recognizing the doctrine of worthier title, the remainder in *G*'s heirs is valid under the Rule Against Perpetuities, because the heirs will be determined at *G*'s death.

d. The remainder in *B* is indefeasibly vested, hence not subject to the Rule Against Perpetuities. The remainder for life in *A*'s children who reach 30, however, is invalid. Being invalid, it is struck out. This accelerates *B*'s remainder: the transfer reads in effect "to *A* for life, remainder to *B*." *B*'s remainder thus vests in possession at *A*'s death.

Parts II and III

1.a. *X*, *B*, and *C* hold as tenants in common.

b. *H*, *B*, and *C* hold as tenants in common.

c. The land passes through *A*'s probate estate and is subject to *S*'s elective share (or right to dower, in the few states that preserve dower). The remaining portion passes to X-Charity. All recipients hold as tenants in common.

2.a. The transfer severs the tenancy (and the right of survivorship) between *A* and *B* and between *A* and *C*. *X* holds as tenant in common with *B* and with *C*. *B* and *C* hold as joint tenants (with the right of survivorship) with each other.

b. The right of survivorship operates at *A*'s death. *H* receives nothing.

c. Property held by the decedent and one or more third parties in joint tenancy is traditionally not subject to the surviving spouse's elective share or dower. In such a jurisdiction, the land would pass automatically to *B* and *C*, with nothing for *S* or X-Charity. The Uniform Probate Code, however, entitles *S* to an elective share in the joint-tenancy property.

3. *G* has used the language of concurrent estates incorrectly. Joint tenancies have a right of survivorship; tenancies in common do not. A court will have to interpret the language to determine which tenancy *G* intended to create. In so doing, the court may use a canon of construction. This fact-pattern is drawn from *Camp v. Camp*, 220 Va. 595, S.E.2d 243 (1979). Relying on the canon that where two clauses are inconsistent the first one governs, the court in *Camp* held that the parties

received the land as tenants in common. Whether this result accords with *G*'s most probable intention is a question you should ponder.

Part IV

1.a. *G* is the donor. *D* is the donee. The objects are any one or more persons. *T* is the taker in default. The power is presently exercisable, general, and collateral.

b. *G* is the donor. *D* is the donee. The objects are any one or more charities. *T* is the taker in default. The power is presently exercisable, nongeneral, and collateral.

c. *G* is the donor. *A* is the donee. The objects are any one or more charities. *T* is the taker in default. The power is testamentary, nongeneral, and in gross.

d. *G* is the donor. *A* is the donee. The only object is *B*. The taker in default is X-Charity. The power is presently exercisable and nongeneral. With respect to the remainder interest, the power is in gross. With respect to *A*'s income interest, the power is appendant and invalid.

2. *G*'s creditors: under modern law, they are entitled to reach the trust assets, because a reserved power to revoke is the same as a reserved general power of appointment. *D*'s creditors: the majority view is that they are not able to reach the property, because *D* did not exercise the power. *D*'s surviving spouse: the traditional view is that the elective share is limited to the decedent's probate estate, which excludes property subject to a presently exercisable general power of appointment; the Uniform Probate Code reaches the opposite result in § 2-205(1)(i).

INDEX

References are to Pages

FEE TAIL
See also Particular Estates; Rule in Shelley's Case
Defined, 23
Present status, 24

FORCED SHARE
See Surviving Spouse

FORFEITURES
Disfavored, 41

FRAGMENTATION OF OWNERSHIP
Generally, 2-4, 6-7
Numerus clausus principle, 4-6

FREEHOLD ESTATES
See also Destructibility Rule; Remainders; Rule in
Shelley's Case
Defined, 17
Types of, 17

FUTURE INTERESTS GENERALLY
Distinction between nonreversionary and reversionary, 32
Importance of, 7-9
Nature of, 3-4

HEIRS
See also Alienability; Class Gifts; Contingent Interests;
Expectancy; Guardian Ad Litem; Inheritance
Presumptive meaning, 165
Primogeniture, 219
Technical meaning for doctrine or worthier title, see
Worthier Title Doctrine

ABOUT THE AUTHORS

Lawrence W. Waggoner is the Lewis M. Simes Professor of Law at the University of Michigan. He is the Reporter for the Restatement (Third) of Property (Wills and Other Donative Transfers) (in process) and the Director of Research of the Joint Editorial Board for Uniform Trust and Estate Acts. He was the principal architect and draftsperson of the 1990 revisions of the Uniform Probate Code. He also served as Reporter for several other uniform acts, including the Uniform Statutory Rule Against Perpetuities (1986), the Revised Uniform Testamentary Additions to Trusts Act (1991), and the Revised Uniform Simultaneous Death Act (1991). He is also an Adviser to the Restatement (Third) of Trusts (in process).

Thomas P. Gallanis is Professor of Law, Professor of History, and Director of the Center for Law and History at Washington and Lee University. He teaches courses in property, trusts and estates (basic and advanced), estate and gift taxation, elder law, and English and European legal history. He is a member of the American Law Institute and participates in the Consultative Groups for the Restatement (Third) of Property (Wills and Other Donative Transfers), the Restatement (Third) of Trusts, and the Principles of the Law of Nonprofit Organizations.